JUNIOR GIRL SCOUT
HANDBOOK

Girl Scouts of the U.S.A.

420 Fifth Avenue

New York, N.Y. 10018

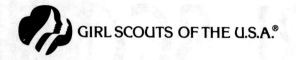
GIRL SCOUTS OF THE U.S.A.®

B. LaRae Orullian, *National President*

Mary Rose Main, *National Executive Director*

Inquiries related to the *Junior Girl Scout Handbook* should be directed to Membership and Program, Girl Scouts of the U.S.A., 420 Fifth Avenue, New York, N.Y. 10018

© 1994 by Girl Scouts of the United States of America

All rights reserved

First Impressions 1994

Printed in the United States of America

ISBN 0-88441-281-4

10   9   8   7

This book is printed on recyclable paper.

Credits

Authors
Chris Bergerson, Judith Brucia, Janice Cummings, Martha Jo Dennison, Toni Eubanks, Joan W. Fincutter, Sharon Woods Hussey, Harriet S. Mosatche, Ph.D., Robyn Payne, Verna Simpkins, Karen Unger-Sparks, Candace White-Ciraco, Ed.D.

Editor
Janet Lombardi

Designer
Kaeser and Wilson Design Ltd.

Illustrators
People: Larry Raymond, pp. 14, 27, 35, 37, 43, 46, 47, 74, 87
How to's: Liz Wheaton, pp. 88, 89, 102, 138, 153, 156, 157, 158, 159, 164, 166, 167, 169, 170, 182, 183, 185, 186, 187, 188, 191
"Jamela the Future Scientist" Cartoon: Sandra Shap, pp. 112-113
Digital Illustrations: Lisa Halter-Park, pp. 18, 58, 75, 79, 80, 82, 86, 100, 103, 105, 107, 118, 119, 152, 153, 160, 161, 176, 177, 178, 179, 180, 181, 183, 185, 187, 188, 190, 191; Ruby Levesque, pg. 172; Carl Van Brunt, pp. 20-21, 38, 93, 148, 150
From Other Girl Scout Sources: Michael Hostovich, pg. 94; Robert Lawson, pp. 13, 130; Linda Reilly, pp. 139-141; Claire Sieffert, pg. 92; Frank Steiner, pp. 10-11; Cornelius Van Wright, pg. 83

Photographers
Cover: Eugene Weisberg
Fashion Shots: Anthony Edgeworth, pp. 16-17
Chapter Lead-in's (bottom photo): Ameen Howrani, pp. 7, 31, 75, 97, 121, 145, 193; Terri Cluck, pg. 131
Other: Ameen Howrani, pp. 60, 75, 121, 149, 184, 192; Ken Korsh, pg. 78; Rex Wilson, pp. 98,101; Joel Wolsson, pg.190; © Stock Market (Peter Beck, Edgeworth Productions, Richard Gross, Blaine Harrington, Henley & Savage, Marcia Keegan, Roy Morsch, Susan Oristaglio, Gabe Palmer, Claudia Parks, Jose Pelaez, J. Pinderhughes, Patti & Milt Putnam, John M. Roberts, William Roy, David Sailors, Ben Simmons, Joe Sohm, Paul Steel, William Whitehurst, Joel Wolfson, Gerald Zanetti), pp. 28, 29, 30, 53, 54, 55, 62, 63, 68, 69, 70, 71, 72, 114, 121(top), 128, 129, 131 (top), 135, 136, 137, 145 (top), 168, 173

CONTENTS

INTRODUCTION

Congratulations on becoming a Junior Girl Scout! Whether you've just joined or you've bridged from Brownie Girl Scouts, you're about to enter a world of fun, friends, and adventures.

This is your handbook filled with stories about girls like you, activities, games, and facts about growing up. In this book you'll learn about camping and the outdoors, staying safe and healthy, protecting the environment, enjoying time with friends and family, playing sports, enjoying the arts and sciences, and much more. You'll also learn about belonging to Girl Scouts of the U.S.A., the largest organization for girls in the country.

Some of your handbook activities you can plan and do with friends and some you will probably want to do on your own. The activities—things to make and do—help you learn more about yourself and what is important to you.

You can write in your handbook, take notes, draw pictures, or attach things to the pages. The chapters do not have to be read in any special order. Your Girl Scout leader can work with you to decide which chapters to read and activities to do. She can help find resources, too, that you might need when doing the activities. She can even suggest other ways of doing the activities.

As you read, you may notice symbols that appear more than once. You will see that some activities appear with a badge symbol that looks like this:

This means that those activities can be done as a badge requirement. In other words, if you finish the activity, you'd be working on earning a badge.

Some other challenging activities are marked like this:

Some activities may require you to take safety precautions or be extra careful. These activities are marked by:

Also, to help you find things in this book quickly, there is an alphabetical index at the end.

Note:

Some badge activities are scattered throughout the chapters, but all badge activities are listed in Chapter Eight. Chapter Eight also has information about other recognitions such as Junior Girl Scout signs.

Why not explore the activities in your handbook? Try this activity treasure hunt.

You need: A *Junior Girl Scout Handbook* for every two girls, paper, and pencils.

With a partner, create a list of ten things that you both guess will be in the handbook. For example: a song, a ceremony, the Girl Scout Promise, a game, a badge, a safety tip, something that helps the environment.

Then, exchange your list for the list of another pair so that you will be working from a new list. Find each item in the handbook and write down the page number where it appears. Each pair then shares their list with the entire group and chooses one activity to do or learn more about.

WELCOME TO GIRL SCOUTING
CHAPTER 1

Who Can Be a Girl Scout?
page 13

The Junior Girl Scout Uniform
page 16

The Girl Scout Pyramid: Where Do You Fit In?
page 20

Camping, Service, and Trips
page 27

Now that you're a Junior Girl Scout, you follow in a long tradition of girls who've made the Girl Scout Promise. Since 1912, girls just like you have had fun making new friends, trying new activities, and helping in their communities.

In this chapter you'll learn how Girl Scouting began and about things like ceremonies, your uniform, and what Junior Girl Scouts do. You'll also learn about the woman who started Girl Scouting—Juliette Gordon Low or Daisy—who was curious and energetic as a child. She loved animals, the outdoors, and playing with her brothers, sisters, and cousins. Well, let her tell you herself…

A Letter from Daisy

My darling Mama,

I rise at six, study an hour before breakfast which is at eight. During the morning I have nothing but French studies. At twelve we have lunch. Three times a week I go to my drawing. I wish you could see my teacher. He is a perfect character. On Saturday morning I go with five other girls from here to Dodsworth's dancing school where they are so swell, but I like it and know already lots of people there.

Daisy

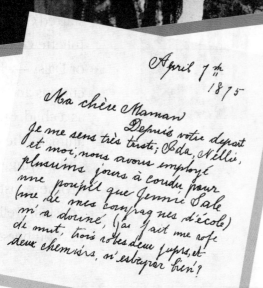

Most of you may know me as the founder of Girl Scouts of the U.S.A. But I imagine very few of you know much about me as a girl your age. I'm sure I wasn't much different from many of you.

I attended boarding school over 100 years ago in New York City, and that letter is one of hundreds I wrote throughout my life. In fact, before telephones, letter writing was the way people kept in touch.

MORE ABOUT DAISY LOW

My full name is Juliette Magill Kinzie Gordon Low. I was born on October 31, 1860, a few months before the Civil War began. My birthday fell on Halloween.

I was named after my grandmother Kinzie, but she was the only one who called me Juliette. When my father wrote to his family in Chicago about me, one of my uncles exclaimed, "I'll bet she'll be a Daisy!" And I remained "Daisy" to my family and to many of my close friends all my life.

I was part of a large family who played and had fun together. I loved animals of all kinds and had some pretty unusual ones. My pet parrot and mockingbird were two of my favorites.

Low

Drawing was my favorite subject in school, and I was good at learning foreign languages. But spelling and arithmetic gave me problems. At times I was too active and fun-loving to sit still in school. My mother wrote: "I send a list of your words (spelled) wrong and the right way to spell them. Please study them hard, as you frequently, in fact, always, spell them wrongly."

Daisy's Spelling	Right Way
sleave	sleeve
idear	idea
disgrase	disgrace
suspence	suspense

I really enjoyed writing plays and acting them out with my brothers and sisters and cousins, and I also made paper dolls by drawing pictures of characters in storybooks and of famous actresses. You can see them today if you visit my home in Savannah.

I also enjoyed learning how to dance. If I were alive today, I would probably know all the latest dance steps. In the 1870s I went to dancing school to learn ballroom dancing. The polka was popular then. In those days, girls were taught more than how to dance. They had to learn how to enter a ballroom, how to curtsy, and most importantly, how to sit properly in a chair. Legs must never be crossed and both feet should rest on the floor. Our skirts had to be arranged in folds, just right. Boys had to learn how to make a formal bow and offer their arms to a partner.

November 8th

Oh Mama!
I feel perfectly miserable, because your going to give me an awful scolding and I know I deserve it. I've lost my beautiful little ring with the blue forgetmenots on it, that Uncle Julian sent fr Europe to me !!!
This is the way I lost it. Percy lent me his gold pen to wear around my neck ribbon, and I lent him m ring (I know you will say "the little fool" but Mama I ex-pect you lent your rings to boys when you were a girl) and of course I didn't know he would lose it, but he did and he felt awfully about it

As Daisy Grew

*S*avannah, Georgia, is very hot during the summers, and people in those days were afraid of catching yellow fever, a dreadful disease. So Mama and Papa sent us children to spend the summer with our Aunt Eliza, my cousin Caroline's mother, in Etowah Cliffs, Georgia. This was further north and much cooler than Savannah.

There was plenty of room in the big house. Sometimes as many as 20 cousins were there at one time. The boys slept on mattresses on the floor, and we girls slept on beds in the bedrooms. During the day, we played in fruit orchards, rose gardens, woods, and the countryside full of wild flowers.

Etowah Cliffs
November 8, 1876

Oh Mama!

I feel perfectly miserable, because you're going to give me an awful scolding and I know I deserve it. I've lost my beautiful little ring with the blue forget-me-nots on it that Uncle Julian sent from Europe to me!!!

This is the way I lost it. Percy lent me his gold pencil to wear around my neck on ribbon, and I lent him my ring (I know you will say "the little fool" but I expect you lent your rings to boys when you were a girl) and of course I didn't know he would lose it, but he did and he felt awfully about it....

Your prodigal daughter,

Daisy

On December 21, 1886, when I was 26 years old, I married an Englishman named Willy Low. I carried lilies of the valley in my wedding bouquet, the favorite flower of my sister Alice who had died. I had already lost some hearing in one of my ears. As I was leaving the ceremony, a piece of rice landed in my good ear and the doctor who removed the grain of rice punctured my eardrum. Eventually, I became almost totally deaf.

*T*hough our marriage got off to a hopeful start, Willy and I became very unhappy. We had a good life in England with lots of friends, but our marriage was not successful and we separated. We had decided to divorce when Willy got very ill and died.

How Girl Scouting Came About

Scout in the United States. She loved to play basketball. In 1912, girls wore enormous pleated gymnasium bloomers to play basketball. They had to cover themselves with overcoats that reached their ankles to cross the street to reach the basketball lot. Before taking off their overcoats, they pulled together huge canvas curtains strung on wires which surrounded the basketball field. That way, nobody could see their bloomered legs from the street!

I was 52 years old and not in good physical health when I made the long boat trip home from England. I could have stayed in England. I had my sculpture and art and friends, but I had learned about an organization that was so exciting that I had to return home to share it with girls in the United States.

I had become friends with Lord Baden-Powell who founded the Boy Scouts. His sister Agnes was in charge of the girls who wanted to make their own Scout troops. They were called Girl Guides. Lord Baden-Powell told me that "there are little stars that guide us on, although we do not realize it." I thought about this saying while I was deciding what I should do next and the direction seemed clear: start Girl Scouts in the United States.

My niece, who was also named Daisy Gordon, was the first Girl

*T*oday, Girl Scouts continue many of the same traditions and activities we did when there were only 3,000 Girl Scouts in 1916. There are almost three million Girl Scouts from all parts of the United States, and there are many more Girl Scouts or Girl Guides in over 100 countries around the world and each has a Girl Scout Promise. Girl Scouts travel, go camping, and become leaders in their communities. They develop a set of values to help guide their actions and they plan many kinds of activities that are fun and different from what they might usually do. But most importantly, Girl Scouts learn how to work with and support each other and have a great time.

Being a Junior Girl Scout

The Girl Scout Promise

On my honor, I will try:
To serve God and my country,
To help people at all times,
And to live by the Girl Scout Law.

The Girl Scout Promise and Law

All Girl Scouts, both girls and adults, make the Girl Scout Promise and agree to try to live by the Girl Scout Law.

Write down what each line of the Promise means to you and discuss what you've written in your troop or group.

On my honor, I will try:
(What does honor mean?)

To serve God
(To go along with their beliefs, some girls may choose to say a word or phrase other than God. What are some ways you can live by your beliefs?)

and my country,
(What are some ways you can serve your country?)

To help people at all times,
(What are some ways you can help people?)

And to live by the Girl Scout Law.
(What are some other words that mean "to live by"?)

An important word or phrase is highlighted on each line of the Girl Scout Law. These words represent the personal characteristics of a Girl Scout. In pairs, choose one line of the Girl Scout Law and tell what the words mean to each of you.

Once the two of you have discussed your words, prepare a demonstration of the word or phrase for the rest of your troop or group. For example, perform a skit or pantomime, write a poem or a make-believe diary entry, draw a picture or make up a telephone conversation about your word. You could ask others to guess what your word or phrase is.

Using the words from the Girl Scout Promise and Law, create a word search, crossword puzzle, or other word game. Exchange your word puzzles with each other and try them out. Put them together to form a word puzzle book. Exchange with other Junior Girl Scout troops or with troops of Brownie Girl Scouts.

The Girl Scout Law*

I will do my best to be
honest and fair,
friendly and helpful,
considerate and caring,
courageous and strong, and
responsible for what
I say and do,
and to
respect myself and others,
respect authority,
use resources wisely,
make the world a better
place, and
be a sister to every
Girl Scout.

(*Adopted by the National Council
at its October 1996 session.)

Who Can Be a Girl Scout?

Any girl who is 5 through 17 years old or in kindergarten through the twelfth grade can become a Girl Scout in the United States. Girls of different races, cultures, and religious groups are welcome in Girl Scouting. Every Girl Scout is expected to make the Girl Scout Promise and try to live by the Girl Scout Law.

The five age levels in Girl Scouting are:

Daisy Girl Scouts
ages 5-6 or grades K, 1

Brownie Girl Scouts
ages 6, 7, 8 or grades 1, 2, 3

Junior Girl Scouts
ages 8, 9, 10, 11
or grades 3, 4, 5, 6

Cadette Girl Scouts
ages 11, 12, 13, 14
or grades 6, 7, 8, 9

Senior Girl Scouts
ages 14, 15, 16, 17
or grades 9, 10, 11, 12

Girl Scout Traditions

As a Junior Girl Scout not only do you get to try fun activities, but you get to be part of a group.

Juliette Low understood how special words and signs help girls feel they are members of a group. Girl Scouts and Girl Guides all

The Girl Scout motto is "Be prepared."

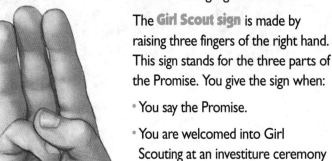

around the world share special signs, a handshake, the friendship squeeze, a motto, and a slogan. These special signs overcome barriers of language and culture.

The **Girl Scout sign** is made by raising three fingers of the right hand. This sign stands for the three parts of the Promise. You give the sign when:

* You say the Promise.

* You are welcomed into Girl Scouting at an investiture ceremony (see page 14).

* You receive a patch or badge.

* You greet other Girl Scouts and Girl Guides.

The **Girl Scout handshake** is a formal way of greeting other Girl Scouts and Girl Guides. You shake hands with the left hand and give the Girl Scout sign with your right hand.

The **quiet sign** is used in meetings and other gatherings to let people know it is time to stop talking. The sign is made by raising your right hand high. As people in the group see the quiet sign, they stop talking and also raise their hands. Once everyone is silent, the meeting continues.

The Girl Scout slogan is "Do a good turn daily."

The **friendship circle** stands for an unbroken chain of friendship with Girl Scouts and Girl Guides all around the world. Girl Scouts and leaders stand in a circle. Each person crosses her right arm over her left and clasps hands with her friends on both sides. Everyone makes a silent wish as a **friendship squeeze** is passed from hand to hand. Form a friendship circle with the girls in your group and try the friendship squeeze.

Ceremonies in Girl Scouting

Many Girl Scouts at all age levels enjoy planning ceremonies. The best ones are created around a theme such as nature, heritage, friendship, or beauty. People express these themes in many ways: through music, songs, stories, poetry, dance, and light. And some ceremonies use common symbols such as a bridge for crossing over, a dove and olive branch for peace, and green plants for nature.

Important times for ceremonies in Girl Scouting are:

Bridging: welcomes girls into another level of Girl Scouts.

Rededication: helps girls think about the meaning of their Girl Scout Promise and Law.

Court of Awards: gives recognition to girls who have accomplished something (such as completing a service project, helping someone, or earning badges).

Flag Ceremonies: are part of any program that honors the American flag.

Fly-Up: a bridging ceremony for Brownie Girl Scouts who are bridging to Junior Girl Scouts.

Special Girl Scout Days: such as the Girl Scout Birthday or Thinking Day.

Investiture: girls welcome someone into Girl Scouting for the first time.

Girl Scouts' Own: an inspirational, girl-planned program to express girls' deepest feelings about something.

Ceremony Worksheet

Name of Ceremony _____

Purpose or Theme _____

Date of Ceremony _____ **Time** _____

Place of Ceremony _____ **Length** _____

Who will attend? _____

How will the ceremony begin? _____
_____

What songs, poems, quotations will be included? _____
_____

What activities will be included in the main part of the ceremony? Will people speak? Will badges or other awards be given? _____
_____

How will the ceremony end? _____

Who will do each part? _____
_____

Who will record the ceremony for your troop's archives or records?_____

What decorations or props are needed? _____

Who will bring the items?

Item(s)	Who Will Bring Them?
_____	_____
_____	_____
_____	_____

What refreshments will be served? _____
_____

Who will bring them? _____

What will refreshments cost? _____

Who will pay for them? _____

When will a rehearsal be scheduled for the ceremony? _____

15

Girl Scouts' Special Days

Girl Scouts in the U.S.A. have four special days that are celebrated all across the nation. Girls often plan events or hold special ceremonies to celebrate these days:

October 31–Juliette Gordon Low's Birthday (also known as Founder's Day)

February 22–Thinking Day, the birthday of both Lord Baden-Powell and Lady Baden-Powell. Girl Scouts and Girl Guides all over the world celebrate this day in international friendship and world peace.

March 12–The birthday of Girl Scouting in the United States of America–celebrated on or as close to the day as possible.

April 22–Girl Scout Leader's Day, when girls show their leaders how much they appreciate them.

The Girl Scout Pin

Your Girl Scout pin shows others that you are a member of Girl Scouts of the U.S.A. Its shape is called a "trefoil," and represents the three parts of the Girl Scout Promise. There are two versions of the membership pin. The newer one has three profiles inside the trefoil. The dark and light profiles represent the ethnic diversity (all the different races and ethnic groups) of Girl Scout membership, and the equal value placed on all girls.

The older version of the pin has the initials "GS" inside the trefoil, along with the American eagle and shield that are part of the Great Seal of the United States of America.

Your World Trefoil Pin

Your blue and gold World Trefoil pin shows that you are part of a worldwide movement of Girl Guides and Girl Scouts. The blue stands for the sky and the gold stands for the sun. The trefoil stands for the three parts of the Girl Scout Promise. The base of the trefoil is shaped like a flame, which represents the love of humanity and the flame that burns in the hearts of Girl Guides and Girl Scouts around the world. The line in the middle of the trefoil stands for the compass needle that guides us, while the two stars stand for the Promise and Law.

16

The Junior Girl Scout Uniform

Just like wearing your Girl Scout pin, wearing a uniform is another way of showing that you belong to an organization. Your uniform was designed with the comments and suggestions of Junior Girl Scouts around the country. It is not a requirement that all Girl Scouts own a uniform. Girls who have one like to wear it to participate in ceremonies, attend an event as part of a Girl Scout group, attend an event on a special Girl Scout day, or attend regular meetings.

The Junior Girl Scout uniform has different pieces that you can mix or match. These pictures show the different styles of the Junior Girl Scout uniform.

Wearing Your Girl Scout Insignia and Recognitions

Girl Scout insignia are the pins that identify you as a Girl Scout. Recognitions are what you earn by doing activities such as earning a badge from the book *Girl Scout Badges and Signs*. They stand for what you have accomplished and earned in Girl Scouting. See the illustrations below and on page 19 that show the correct placement of your insignia and recognitions on a sash or vest.

Girl Scouts USA identification strip
Council identification strip
Troop crest
Troop numerals
Membership stars
Bridge to Junior Girl Scouts patch
Junior Aide patch
Junior Girl Scout Leadership pin
Religious recognitions, lifesaving awards, other special pins and awards, and/or insignia of other groups. Worn below membership stars or to left of Bridge to Junior Girl Scouts patch.

Patrol leader's cord
World Trefoil pin
Girl Scout membership pin
Numeral guard
Sign of the Rainbow, Sign of the Sun, Sign of the Satellite, and Sign of the World
Brownie Girl Scout Wings
Girl Scout Proficiency badges

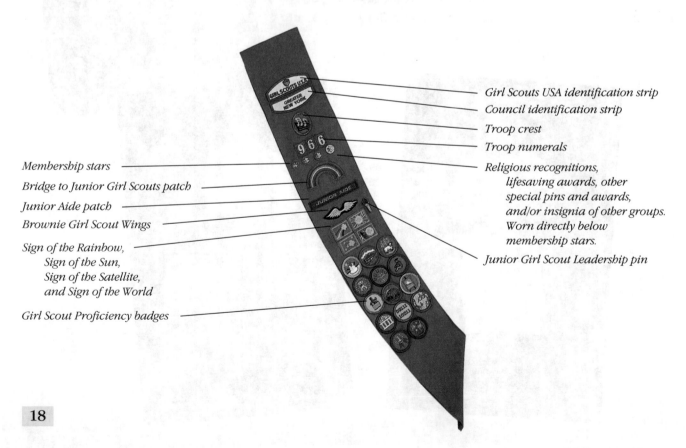

Membership stars
Bridge to Junior Girl Scouts patch
Junior Aide patch
Brownie Girl Scout Wings
Sign of the Rainbow, Sign of the Sun, Sign of the Satellite, and Sign of the World
Girl Scout Proficiency badges

Girl Scouts USA identification strip
Council identification strip
Troop crest
Troop numerals
Religious recognitions, lifesaving awards, other special pins and awards, and/or insignia of other groups. Worn directly below membership stars.
Junior Girl Scout Leadership pin

Insignia/Recognition Guide

  Girl Scout membership pin

 Brownie Girl Scout Wings

 World Trefoil pin

 Special awards
Religious recognitions, lifesaving awards and other special pins may be worn below the membership stars.

 Insignia tab
Can be used to hold your World Trefoil and Girl Scout membership pins.

Badges
On the sash, these are placed three in a row. On the vest, the first three are placed on the right side. Most badges will be worn on the left side because there is more space, but you can create additional rows on the right side.

  Patrol leader's cord

 Girl Scouts USA identification strip

Sign of the Rainbow, Sign of the Sun, Sign of the Satellite, Sign of the World
Worn in two rows with Sign of the Rainbow and Sign of the Satellite on your right.

Council identification strip

 Troop crest

 Junior Girl Scout leadership pin

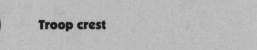 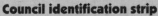 **Troop numerals**

Note
Girl Scout patches from events, camp, or projects may be worn on the back of the sash beginning at the top. Badges that will not fit on the front of the sash may be placed on the back of the sash beginning on the bottom. Try-It patches earned as a Brownie Girl Scout may also be placed here.

 Membership stars and discs
(One for each year in Girl Scouting) worn directly below the troop numerals, beginning with the Daisy Girl Scout star on a blue disc, Brownie Girl Scout stars on green discs, then Junior Girl Scout stars on yellow discs.

 Bridge to Junior Girl Scout's patch

 Junior Aide patch

 In your troop or group, divide into two teams. Each team should have the exact same set of insignia and recognitions. You could have a relay race to see which team can place its set of recognitions/insignia on a sash or vest correctly in the least amount of time. You could try this by yourself using a timer to see how quickly you can place the recognitions in the correct spots.

The Girl Scout Pyramid

Many people in Girl Scouting help make your Girl Scout experience successful. Look at the Girl Scout pyramid. You are at the top of the pyramid. Write your name. You and millions of other girls—around this nation and around the world—are the reasons that Girl Scouting exists.

One way to take part in Girl Scouting is to join a troop. If you are in a Girl Scout troop, put your troop number in the next part of the pyramid. If you are not part of a troop, write in the names of the friends with whom you do Girl Scout activities.

Adults in Girl Scouting

Adults help you carry out Girl Scout activities. They could be: Girl Scout leaders, volunteers who work with Girl Scout troops or groups, or other adults such as family members. Write in the names of the adults who work with your troop or group. If you are not part of a troop or group, write in the names of those special adults who help you with Girl Scout activities.

A Girl Scout council is a group of women and men who administer Girl Scouting in a specific area. These people have many different jobs. They may help start new troops, take care of camps, or sign up new members. There are more than 300 councils in the United States today. Find out the name of your Girl Scout council and write it on the pyramid. You can wear the name of your council on your uniform sash or vest. (See page 18.)

Next on the pyramid is Girl Scouts of the U.S.A. (GSUSA), the national organization. The membership dues that you pay to GSUSA each year provide services to members. GSUSA creates new program activities and books, like this handbook, and operates national centers (see page 22). GSUSA also coordinates national and international events, such as wider opportunities for Cadette and Senior Girl Scouts. Turn to page 27 to learn more about wider opportunities.

HANDBOOK ACTIVITY Invite someone who knows about your council office to a Girl Scout meeting to talk about what she does and how the council operates.

Girl Scouts

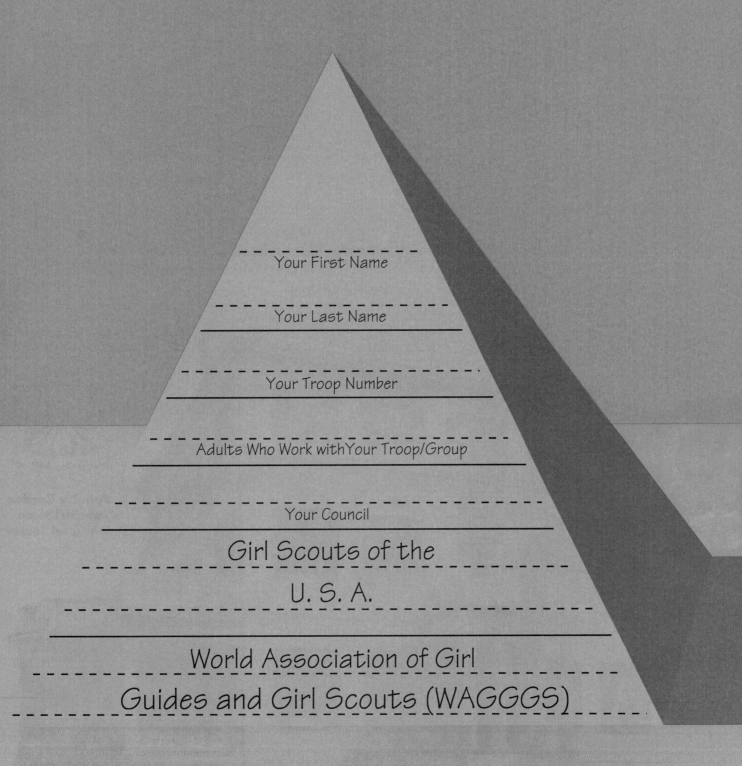

Your First Name

Your Last Name

Your Troop Number

Adults Who Work with Your Troop/Group

Your Council

Girl Scouts of the

U. S. A.

World Association of Girl

Guides and Girl Scouts (WAGGGS)

The National Centers

Edith Macy Conference Center

Girl Scouts of the U.S.A. owns two Girl Scout national centers, each with its own special activities.

Juliette Gordon Low Girl Scout National Center, in Savannah, Georgia, is the childhood home of the founder of Girl Scouting in the United States. Many troops visit each year. You can receive more information by writing to Juliette Gordon Low Girl Scout National Center, 142 Bull Street, Savannah, Georgia 31401.

At Edith Macy Conference Center, 35 miles from New York City, adults take classes to learn more about Girl Scouting. Camp Andree Clark, GSUSA's camp, is nearby.

Juliette Gordon Low Girl Scout National Center

The World Association of Girl Guides & Girl Scouts (WAGGGS)

At the base of the pyramid is the World Association of Girl Guides and Girl Scouts (WAGGGS). Your World Trefoil pin shows that you are a part of this growing worldwide movement.

Each of the national Girl Scout/Girl Guide organizations, including Girl Scouts of the U.S.A., belongs to the World Association of Girl Guides and Girl Scouts (WAGGGS). This means that because you are a Girl Scout, you are connected to eight million girls and women around the world.

WAGGGS owns four world centers. Our Cabaña is in Cuernavaca, Mexico; Our Chalet is in Adelboden, Switzerland; Pax Lodge is at the Olave Center in London, England; and Sangam is in Pune, India. Through international wider opportunities, Cadette and Senior Girl Scouts can visit these centers and take part in many activities. As a registered Girl Scout, you and your family can also stay at these centers on a visit to these countries if you have made arrangements ahead of time.

For more information, write to
Membership and Program
Girl Scouts of the U.S.A.
420 Fifth Avenue
New York, New York 10018-2702.

Different Ways to Be a Girl Scout

Part of the fun of Girl Scouting is sharing experiences with girls your age. You can do this in many ways. You might be part of a group called the Girl Scout troop. A troop works together to make decisions, to choose activities to do together, and to make sure that everyone's feelings and interests are respected. You might also be part of an interest group, go to a program center, or even do Girl Scout activities by mail or computer.

1. The Patrol System

Troop and Group Leadership

Your Junior Girl Scout troop or group is the perfect place to practice and strengthen your leadership skills. (See Chapter Six for more about leadership.) Along with your Girl Scout leader, you and your troop or group members can set up a system for troop or group government. Within this system, you have different opportunities to take a leadership role.

Here are the three models of troop or group government most used by Junior Girl Scouts. Which system would work best in achieving your troop's or group's goals? What could be your role in troop or group government?

The troop or group is divided into small groups or patrols with five to eight girls in each. If you have 20 girls in your troop or group, how could you divide yourselves into patrols?

You can divide into patrols based on interests, by age, or at random. Because making friends and learning how to work well with others are a big part of Girl Scouting, you should not be in the same patrol an entire troop year.

How does a patrol work? Each patrol usually chooses a patrol leader, an assistant patrol leader, a patrol name, and a patrol symbol. The members of a patrol should rotate the patrol leader and assistant leader jobs so everyone has the opportunity to serve in a leadership role. The patrol name and logo can be used on a patrol flag and on any special patrol materials.

During a special ceremony, the patrol leader is given the patrol leader cord, a recognition made up of two gold cord loops or circles, to wear on her left shoulder. The larger circle symbolizes the whole troop or group while the smaller circle represents the patrol.

The patrol leader is usually responsible for seeing that certain jobs are done. Some of these jobs can be organizing the patrol, helping new members, keeping patrol records, leading discussions, and representing the patrol at the Court of Honor meetings.

In Girl Scouting, a job is called a kaper and a list of jobs and who does them is a kaper chart. See the next page for an example.

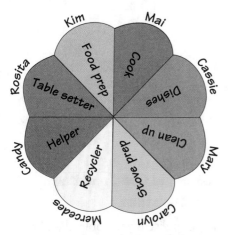

This kaper chart is one Girl Scouts might use for camping

The patrol leader wouldn't do all these jobs herself. She works with the girls in her patrol to get everything accomplished.

The assistant patrol leader is usually responsible for assisting the patrol leader during meetings and taking over patrol meetings in her absence.

Court of Honor

The Girl Scout leader, the patrol leaders, and the troop or group secretary and treasurer make up the Court of Honor. The secretary takes notes at troop or group meetings and keeps these notes as a record of what was discussed. The treasurer tracks troop or group dues and other Girl Scout money and supplies. In some large troops and groups, patrols might have secretaries and treasurers who do these jobs in the patrols. At Court of Honor meetings, held before or after regular troop or group meetings, the Court of Honor might come

up with plans or ideas for the patrols to discuss and vote on, ask for ideas and suggestions from patrols, and set up and maintain a troop kaper chart that outlines assignments for each patrol.

If you are not on the Court of Honor, attend a meeting when it is open to all members because it will give you an opportunity to see leadership in action.

2. The Executive Board System

In this type of troop government, you do not have small group patrols. There is one leadership team for the whole troop or group called an executive board. This system often works well with smaller troops and groups. (In some troops, this group is called the steering committee.) The board's main responsibility is to help make plans and assign jobs for the entire troop or group based on interests and needs.

The executive board usually has a president, a vice-president, a secretary, and a treasurer, and holds its own meetings to discuss troop or group matters. The length of time each girl can be on the executive board should be limited so that during the year all members of the

troop or group get an opportunity to participate. All of the girls in the troop or group decide on a way at the beginning of the year to pass their ideas and suggestions to the executive board. The number of officers on the executive board can vary.

3. The Town Meeting System

In this system, there is no formal group or troop government. Troop and group business is discussed and decided at meetings attended by all the girls in the troop or group. And as in the other systems, everyone in the troop gets the chance to participate in decision-making and leadership.

This system usually requires a moderator, a person who guides a discussion. She makes sure that everyone gets a chance to speak, that no one talks for too long, and that all ideas get considered. How do you choose a moderator? You could pick one girl at random, rotate the job, or select the person who knows the most about the topic. You also need to decide whether or not a secretary and a treasurer need to be elected and how long each would serve.

Group Decision-Making

Sometimes it can be hard to make decisions as a group. How do you decide which service project to do or which trip to take? Here are some decision-making steps:

1. Brainstorm

Brainstorming is a way to get a group of people to talk about a lot of different ideas in a short time. For example, you can brainstorm a solution to a problem, ideas for activities, or suggestions for a trip. Here's how it works: a group usually sits in a circle; one person writes down everybody's ideas. A timer can be set to limit the brainstorming to two minutes, five minutes, or whatever is decided. Then, as people think of ideas, they say them. None of the ideas should be judged good, bad, possible, or impossible until the time is up. Everyone should feel free to say whatever pops into her mind. When the time is up, the group reviews the list of ideas to pick one or two possibilities.

2. Look at the Good and Bad Points of Each Idea

Have a group discussion about the ideas on your brainstormed list.

3. Make a Decision

If, after reviewing the good and bad points, one idea doesn't stand out as the best, the group may want to vote. Vote secretly by ballot or less formally by raising hands.

4. Evaluate

After a decision has been made, the troop or group should discuss their feelings about it at a later date. Is it time for a new decision?

Choosing Leaders

Whenever you choose girls as leaders, think about how you are making your choices. Think about being fair. Think about what it takes to be a leader. For more ideas, look at Chapter Six, which has lots of information about leadership styles.

Camping, Service, and Trips:
Three Favorite Girl Scout Activities

Camping

Camping is a favorite activity for many Girl Scouts, especially troop or group camping at council sites or at summer resident or day camps.

If you haven't gone before, you may be worried about your first camping experience. Bugs, no TV, no flush toilets, and cold showers might be just a few of your worries. "Roughing it is all very fine to talk about, but it's best to make your camp as comfortable as possible" was advice given the first Girl Scouts in their *Handbook for Girl Scouts*. Today, most girls new to camping stay in lodges, cabins, or four-walled tents with access to showers and flush toilets. Read pages 177–192 for more information on camping.

Community Service

Some of the activities you and your troop members discuss may involve providing service to others. Service means doing something helpful for others without expecting or asking for money or any other reward. Service is an important part of Girl Scouting. Read more about leadership and service in Chapter Six.

Wider Opportunities

A wider opportunity is any activity that you and your Girl Scout friends participate in outside of the troop meeting. Visiting a farm, camping, marching in a parade, or having

a picnic away from where you usually meet are all examples of wider opportunities. Participating in wider opportunities as a Junior Girl Scout can help you grow and prepare for greater challenges.

Sometimes people think that wider opportunities refer only to those events that appear each year in the booklet *Wider Ops* and are open only to Cadette and Senior Girl Scouts. But, Junior Girl Scouts have lots of choices for wider opportunities. Brainstorm a list of wider opportunities for your group or troop.

 Invite a Cadette or Senior Girl Scout or someone from your Girl Scout council to talk to you and your friends about a wider opportunity. Find out which events and workshops you can attend as a Junior Girl Scout.

 Learn about wider opportunities now being offered by Girl Scout councils. Ask your Girl Scout leader to see if she can bring a copy of *Wider Ops* to a troop or group meeting. Look through it and find three wider opportunities you think you would enjoy when you are a Cadette or Senior Girl Scout. Make a list of the requirements, cost, location, and any special equipment you would need to bring.

Get Ready to TAP!

Before you board a bus or buckle your seatbelt, careful planning is essential to ensure the success of your wider opportunities. These steps would also be helpful in planning activities and service projects. (See Chapter Eight for Wider Opportunities badge activities.) What do you do first? Try following the Travel Action Plan (TAP) outlined below. You might need more than one meeting to do all the steps.

TAP Step 1

Listed below are some places you and your friends might like to visit or events you would like to attend. On the blank lines, record some other ideas.

- Library
- Park
- Zoo or wildlife center
- Government office
- Homeless shelter
- Science center
- Country fair

_____
_____
_____
_____
_____

 Write a brief description of a real or an imaginary place you would love to visit!

TAP Step 2

When you have narrowed your list to two or three possible activities, you are now ready to hold a planning meeting. Consider and discuss:

1. What will you do once you arrive?

2. How much will it cost? How can you raise money or get help with the finances?

3. How will you get there?

4. What does each of you need to bring?

5. Will you travel in uniform?

6. How will you get your meals?

7. When is the best time to go? When will you leave? Get home?

8. Do you need to make reservations or get permission to visit the place?

9. Will the weather affect plans?

10. Do you need approval from your Girl Scout council?

11. What guidelines does your leader's copy of *Safety-Wise*, a Girl Scout book that outlines safety guidelines and standards, have for your plans?

12. How many adults need to go along?

Use the results of this meeting to help you make a final decision!

 You just finished your planning meeting for your fantasy trip. Summarize the decisions you made. Use the questions above to help you outline your thoughts.

TAP Step 3

Once you decide where you are going, find out as much as you can about the place you plan to visit. Write or telephone ahead to the place, or write to the visitors' bureau or Chamber of Commerce of the town or city you'll be visiting to obtain local maps or tourist brochures.

 Design a travel brochure for your imaginary place. Include details about any special attractions, places to stay and eat, and weather conditions.

TAP Step 4

Calculate how much the trip will cost. Make a list of everything you expect to pay for and estimate how much each thing will cost. Include meals, transportation, equipment, materials, and admission and/or ticket fees.

 Create a chart or graph that shows what it will cost to visit your fantasy place. Be sure to include the cost of meals, transportation, accommodations (hotels, for example), and fees to visit areas of special interest.

TAP! TAP!

29

TAP! TAP!

TAP Step 5

You must get written permission from your parent or guardian before going on any trip. You must also have enough adults to go with you. Your Girl Scout leader will consult *Safety-Wise*. Your leader will make sure there are permission slips from everyone and the right number of adults to accompany the group on a trip.

 Design a permission slip that girls would have to complete before visiting your fantasy place. Include any special information that you think their parents would need to know.

TAP Step 6

Determine ahead of time special clothing and equipment to bring. It is a good idea to sew name labels in your clothes so they don't get mixed up with other girls' clothes. Learn about rolling or packing clothes to fit into a suitcase, sleeping bag, or knapsack.

 Make a list of clothing, accessories, and special equipment a girl would need to bring to your fantasy place.

TAP Step 7

Review a map or a floor plan of the place you plan to visit to figure out exactly how to get there and where you will go once inside. Remember to bring the map with you on your trip!

 Draw a map of your fantasy place that shows major roads, large bodies of water, points of interest, names of towns, and anything else you think potential visitors might need to know!

TAP Step 8

Once you reach this step, you are ready to make your plans into reality! Have a great time!

 Put together all the pieces of your fantasy TAP package and make a presentation to the other members of your troop. How many girls would like to join you?

As you can see, Junior Girl Scouts get to enjoy all sorts of activities from camping and sports to computers to jewelry making. The choice is yours and so is the fun!

WHO AM I...NOW?

CHAPTER 2

Changes in Your Body

What's Important to You?

Values Check

It's Party Time!

A Fun-to-Read Story Maze

This is a truly exciting time in your life as each day brings new discoveries—about yourself, your family, your friends—and so many things in the world around you. This chapter is titled "Who Am I...Now?" because how you look and feel today may be different from how you looked and felt last year, and how you'll look and feel in a few months or next year. On the following pages, you will be asked to step back and look at yourself both inside and out. You will look at the ways your body is changing and the different feelings you are experiencing. You will explore how these changes shape what you value, including your relationships with your family and friends.

WHO AM I NOW?

Use the chart below or write on a separate piece of paper the ways you have changed in the past year.

Topic   Ways I Have Changed

The Way I Look: _____

_____

_____

Friends: _____

_____

_____

_____

Things I Like to Do: _____

_____

_____

How I Feel About Myself: _____

_____

_____

Things I Do with My Family: _____

_____

_____

Other Changes I Have Noticed: _____

_____

_____

THIS IS ME!

How would you fill in the blanks? You might want to use a separate piece of paper, as your answers could change during your time in Junior Girl Scouts. You might not be able to fill in all of the blanks. That's fine. Just skip ahead to the next one you can do.

My name is_____

and my parents called me this because_____

_____.

One thing I like about my name is_____.

My nickname is_____because_____

_____. I am_____

years old and am in_____grade at

_____School.

I am_____feet_____inches tall, have

_____hair,_____eyes, and weigh

_____pounds. One thing I do really

well is_____

_____.

I enjoy doing this because_____

_____.

To get even better at this, I could_____

_____

I also enjoy_____

and I hope to learn more about_____

_____.

Two things that I don't do as well as I

would like to are:_____

and_____.

Here is a picture of me:
(paste or draw)

Here are some of what I like and dislike:

	Like	Dislike
Food	_____	_____
	_____	_____
Clothes	_____	_____
	_____	_____
Music	_____	_____
	_____	_____
Book	_____	_____
	_____	_____
School subject	_____	_____
	_____	_____
Game/sports	_____	_____
	_____	_____

One thing that makes me feel really good inside is_____

_____. I am also very

happy when _____.

Families come in all shapes and sizes! I have _____ members of my family. _____ live with

me and _____ do not live with me. I have _____ pets. Their names are:_____

_____

I enjoy spending time with my friend, _____. One thing we often do

together is _____ and we love to talk about

_____. We haven't always agreed on everything, though. One time we had

a fight about _____. But we

eventually made up by _____.

And just one more thing I would like to share about myself is_____

_____.

GROWING UP FEMALE

Amy looked over at her sleeping sister. How did Ruthie manage to fall asleep so quickly? "Why am I so different from my sister?" wondered Amy, staring up at the ceiling of the room the two girls shared. Thirteen-year-old Ruthie knew just what she wanted to do when she grew up. She had her whole life planned. She was going to be a lawyer, marry Alex, and have two children. And she had known that since she was about eight. Eleven-year-old Amy, on the other hand, had no idea what she wanted to do or be. But Mom kept telling her she had lots of time to make up her mind.

It's not easy growing up. Your family, your teachers, and your friends expect you to act or look a certain way. You are faced with decisions about school, career, and family.

As a girl, you encounter particular challenges. Some people may think you should only be interested in certain jobs. Others may say that the most important thing is how you look. Or they may say it's not important for you to learn how to use a computer or do complicated math problems.

But being a girl today means that you can be smart and look any way you want. It means that you can be a caring friend and a math whiz. You can fix cars and have a stylish haircut. You can be a great baby-sitter and play a super game of basketball. You are an important person with talents and skills—some you may not have had the time to learn about yet! Opportunities are out there for you to grow up to be the best you can be!

 Interview women of different ages and backgrounds to find out what it was like when they were growing up. Talk to your mother, grandmother, aunt, neighbor, older sister, teacher, or Girl Scout leader. What challenges did they face when they were your age? What were their hopes and dreams? Collect their responses in a journal or on tape. What similar concerns do you have about growing up? What different concerns?

CHANGES

Have you asked yourself: "Am I normal?" Are you quickly outgrowing your clothes? Do your arms and legs seem too long for your body? Do you feel happy one minute and sad the next? Would you rather spend more time with friends than with family members?

If you answered yes to one or more of these questions, you are sharing common feelings and experiences with girls and boys whose bodies are changing and becoming more adult. This period of change is called puberty.

Listen to a conversation between Megan, a ten-year-old Junior Girl Scout, who has been feeling confused about growing up, and her 15-year-old sister, Katrina, who has already experienced many of these changes.

Megan was listening, waiting for Katrina to come back from track practice. Boom! The front door slammed.

"I'm home!" Katrina yelled.

"Great—maybe now is the perfect time...." Megan thought, "I have to talk to her today!"

She stood by the open doorway of Katrina's room. "Can we talk?"

"Sure," Katrina said. "What's going on?" Katrina put her track clothes in her laundry bag and patted the bed. "Sit here. I could use a rest—practice was tough—but I made my fastest time this year!"

"Super—that's great.... I don't know what to ask you first. I was going to talk with Mom, but it's a lot easier to talk with you. Didn't you feel embarrassed talking about stuff when you were my age?"

IN YOUR BODY

"What kind of stuff?" Katrina asked.

"You know—getting your period and growing up stuff," Megan said.

"Yeah, sometimes, and I didn't have an older sister," Katrina said.

"All of my friends at school are talking about getting their periods and wearing bras and I feel like I don't know anything. How did you feel when you were ten?"

"Confused, unsure of myself, I didn't know at first what was going on...but, it's all a part of growing up. Talking about all of this is normal," Katrina said. "And, I found out most of my friends felt the same way. Your body goes through a lot of changes in puberty. And, puberty can start anywhere from 8 to 16 so everyone's going

through it at a different time. I remember in health class, we learned about the body—you know, about things like the pituitary gland and hormones and how they help your body grow and develop."

"What are glands? And what are hormones?" Megan asked.

"Let's see, if I remember, glands are parts of your body that make hormones for the body to use, and hormones are chemicals that travel through the bloodstream and help you to grow and develop. Wow—I can't believe I remembered that!"

"How come some girls have gotten their periods? And I haven't gotten mine yet?"

"Every girl is different. There is no right or

wrong time to begin puberty. And, some of your friends will change really quickly and others more slowly. Some will have larger breasts and others smaller. Do you know when you'll see these changes in your body?"

"No, when?" Megan asked.

"When the time is right for you."

"When did you first notice that you were changing?" Megan asked.

"You have a lot of questions, don't you? Okay... I think I started to perspire more. I remember borrowing Mom's deodorant. I also noticed hair growing under my

arms and near my vagina. My pants and skirts got tight and my breasts felt sore. So, Mom and I went bra shopping! I hated putting on one of those things. Would you believe some boys in class made fun of me? They were such jerks that I never let them bother me," Katrina said.

"I think getting my period will be a lot more embarrassing than wearing a bra," Megan said.

"Not if you know what to expect."

"Like what?"

Getting Your Period

One of the most important changes in your body will be the start of menstruation. An organ in your body called a uterus starts to make a lining that will build up and then shed and pass out of the body through the vagina. This tissue contains blood but you are not really bleeding when the tissue comes out. Menstruation usually begins between ages 9 and 16. It is okay to begin earlier or later.

You may have heard menstruation called "a period." That's because it is a periodic cycle that happens about every 28 days and usually lasts for a period of three to seven days. In the beginning it may be more irregular, though.

The first sign of menstruation is usually a small amount of blood, not a "gushing" of blood. Menstrual pads (sanitary napkins) or tampons can be used to absorb the menstrual flow. Menstrual pads are worn inside underwear. Tampons are worn inside the vagina. The use of pads or tampons is a personal choice that a parent or guardian can help you make.

"I still have a book called *Getting Your Period*. Why don't you read it?" Katrina reached to the shelf above her dresser. Tucked away to the side was a slim booklet, *Getting Your Period*. (See opposite page.)

"Katrina, can I ask just one more question? What about the weird feelings I get? I mean one minute I'm happy and then the next minute I feel like crying...."

"Well, how you feel changes as your body changes. I was so confused. Some days I felt great; other days I felt terrible. And when both happened in one day I thought something was really wrong with me. But my friends and I talked and we realized this was happening to everybody and these feelings were normal. It's really okay to feel embarrassed and concerned about all of these changes."

"Katrina, are the same things happening to boys?"

"Uh-huh, boys are changing too. Boys' voices become deeper. They get taller, grow body hair, and their muscles get larger."

"It's great to have a sister to talk to about these things—and of course, who'll be a famous track star someday, too! Thanks a lot, Sis!"

If you have questions or want information about menstruation and how your body changes during puberty, talk with an adult you trust, like a parent, older sister, teacher, school nurse, Girl Scout leader, or adult friend. Remember, menstruation is a normal, healthy function of the female body. It means you are becoming a young woman and that your body is able to produce a baby.

Get the Facts

How much do you and your friends really know about puberty? Test your knowledge by taking this quiz. Some of the statements are facts and others are myths. Answers are on the next page.

Puberty Fact or Myth?

Answer TRUE if it is a fact and answer FALSE if it is a myth.

1. **Girls shouldn't swim or bathe while they are menstruating.**

2. **It is common for girls beginning to menstruate to skip their period for a few months.**

3. **If a girl isn't menstruating by the time she's 15, there is something wrong with her.**

4. **Having oily skin and pimples is part of growing up for most teenagers.**

5. **Usually, both breasts are exactly the same size and shape.**

6. **A girl can become pregnant before she has her first period.**

7. **Girls usually begin puberty earlier than boys.**

8. **Boys can tell when a girl is having her period.**

9. **All girls have menstrual cramps during their period.**

10. **Young girls should not use tampons.**

Answer Key: Myth and Fact Quiz

1. MYTH. It is fine for girls to swim, and they should bathe or shower when they are having their periods. If a girl chooses to go swimming, she can use a tampon. A girl can also wash her hair. In fact, there is no reason to limit activity during your period.

2. FACT. When girls first start menstruating, they often have irregular cycles. They may skip a month or two at times.

3. MYTH. Absolutely not. A girl may begin her period as early as age eight or as late as sixteen.

4. FACT. Most teenagers will get pimples during adolescence and some into adulthood. There are some teenagers who do not get pimples.

5. MYTH. Most breasts are not the same shape and size. One breast may be a little larger or a little lower than the other.

6. FACT. A girl can become pregnant before she begins menstruating. An egg can leave the ovary before her menstrual cycle begins. It means her body is able to produce a baby, but does not mean that she is ready to handle the physical, emotional, and financial demands of caring for a baby.

7. FACT. Most girls begin puberty one to two years earlier than boys. However, boys do catch up with girls.

8. MYTH. No one will know you have your period unless you tell them. There is nothing to be ashamed of should a boy find out.

9. MYTH. Not everyone gets menstrual cramps. Some girls get cramps in their abdomen or lower back.

10. MYTH. With the help of their parents or guardians, girls can make their own decisions about which sanitary products to use. Young girls can use tampons; those who do will probably prefer to use the slender or junior size.

Why not try some of the activities in the badges Becoming a Teen and My Self-Esteem, or some of the activities in the Girls Are Great: Growing Up Female Contemporary Issues booklet?

Brenda's Advice Column

Brenda is a college student who spends a lot of time giving advice to young people. Below are some letters she has received from girls your age. Read the letters and discuss as a group what advice you would give each girl. Then, look at the answers to find out what advice Brenda gave. Keep in mind there is more than one way to handle each situation.

Dear Brenda:

I haven't gotten my period yet, but I am so nervous that it will happen when I'm at school. What will I do?

Nervous

Dear Brenda:

It seems like everybody else knows I'm growing up except my dad. He thinks he can come into my room anytime. I feel I should have some privacy. What should I do?

Growing Up

Dear Brenda:

There is a boy in my class I really like. He always seems to ignore me. How can I let him know how I feel about him?

Confused

Dear Brenda:

Most of my friends are wearing bras. My mother doesn't think I need to wear one. How can I convince her that I'd feel better if I could wear a bra?

Anxious

Please Note:

You can also visit Dr. M and her daughter, Liz, on GSUSA's website, Just for Girls.

Our address is http://www.gsusa.org

Brenda's Answers

Dear Nervous:

One of the biggest concerns girls have about their period is where they'll be when they get it. To feel more comfortable about getting your period, consider keeping a sanitary pad or supply of tissues in your pocketbook, book bag, or locker so you can be prepared. Understanding ahead of time what will happen can help you feel more comfortable.

Brenda

Dear Growing Up:

You are right. You should have some privacy. It seems like time for you to have a talk with your dad. He needs to be reminded that you are growing up. Let him know exactly how you feel. Let him know that you would prefer that he knock before coming into your room. If you feel uncomfortable talking to your dad or if he doesn't seem to understand, talk to your mom or another adult who can help you communicate your feelings to your dad.

Brenda

Dear Anxious:

Wanting to be like your friends is quite normal. Let your mother know how important it is for you to wear a bra. Let her know that you think you are ready to wear a bra. You might even ask her to go shopping with you to buy one. If she still insists that you do not need one, wait a while and then talk with her again. No matter what happens, the most important thing is that you feel great about the way you look—with or without a bra.

Brenda

Dear Confused:

It is quite normal for boys to ignore girls at this age. If you really want him to know how you feel, you have to tell him. This may not be easy. You could tell him in person, call him on the telephone, give him a note, or have a friend tell him for you. You could even ask him questions to show that you are interested in him. You must decide which way makes you feel the most comfortable. Keep in mind that he may or may not like you. Good luck!

Brenda

BODY IMAGE

It's Monday morning and you stretch before you get out of bed. You feel rested after a good night's sleep. You brush your teeth, comb your hair, and pull on your leggings and an oversized T-shirt. As you turn to grab your books, you take a quick look in the mirror and think

_____ !

Some people look in a mirror and like what they see; others don't. Most people want to look their best, but many times girls believe that to be popular and appreciated by others, they must be beautiful.

What people think of as beautiful is greatly influenced by what they see in magazines, on television, in movies, and in books. (These are different kinds of media.) To find out what the media's definition of beauty is, try the following activities:

 With your troop or group members, gather different types of magazines; include magazines that have a particular focus such as gardening, sports, current events, or women's interests. Then, scan the pages, clipping out pictures of women and men. When you have at least a dozen pictures, spread them out on the floor. According to these pictures, how would you generally describe the following?

•Teeth	•Chest	•Hair
•Legs	•Lips	•Skin color
•Eyes	•Waist	•Arms

Now, separate the magazines by type or topic. Using the list above as a guideline, compare each magazine's definition of beauty. What differences do you notice?

 Keep a television log for one week. Tune in to different programs, including news shows, for approximately 15 minutes. Take notes on the appearances of men, women, and children. Look at hairstyle, clothing, age, skin color, weight, and facial features (eyes, nose, teeth, etc.). At the end of the week, look over your notes. What common characteristics do you notice?

Overall, how do the media define beauty for a female? a male? Do you feel this is realistic? Why or why not?

Feeling Comfortable with Who You Are

Some girls believe that to be beautiful, they must be very thin. In fact, many girls think they weigh too much, and often they are wrong. When they look in the mirror, they see themselves as "fat" or "overweight." They go on diets to become even thinner or exercise excessively. Being very underweight or "too thin" can be dangerous to your health. On the other hand, some girls really are overweight and that is not healthy either. Always check with a doctor or nurse to find out what weight is right for your body type and what you can do to lose or gain weight if necessary.

Feeling good about yourself should not be based on just how you look. First, what is beautiful and attractive to one person may not be to another. Second, the real definition of beauty includes things that you can't always see in someone's face: intelligence, friendliness, kindness, and helpfulness are just a few things that can add to a person's beauty. What else do you feel adds to a person's beauty?

Remember, though, that wanting to change your looks can be healthy at times. If you are really overweight, you may want to lose some weight through exercise and a good diet. You may be wearing braces so that your teeth will be straight. Can you think of some other positive ways to change your looks?

 Prepare a short skit that uses not only words but also pictures, symbols, and body language to deliver one of the following messages: What's special about being a girl? What's exciting about growing up? What's your definition of beauty? Perform your skit for other members of your troop or group and for Daisy and Brownie Girl Scouts.

Tears filled Maria's eyes and she looked down, hoping no one would notice. "I can't believe I said 'no.' I do want to join their game. I don't know why I'm always saying 'no' when I really do want to play with them."

Sherry was about to burst. She couldn't wait until her mom got home so she could share the news—first place in the science fair!

Layla was doing her homework when her mom walked in the door. "Great! You made it home early today—can we go to the store and get those new sneakers I wanted?" Layla's mom said, "Honey, we have to have a serious talk. The reason I'm home early is I got fired from my job."

How do you think you would feel in each of these situations? Then, talk with your friends about some of the situations and describe the feelings: angry, happy, afraid, lonely, proud, worried, disappointed, loved, eager, frustrated, embarrassed, surprised, excited, jealous, sad. You'll probably find that your feelings in certain situations are different from those of your friends. There is no right or wrong way to feel.

"Did Abdul really say that?" Kayla asked her best friend Latifeh. "Yes, he really said that he liked you and that he thought you were pretty," Latifeh answered."

Georgia's mother had been ill with AIDS for many months. She would probably die within days, the doctor said. Georgia reached out to hold her mother's hand.

Migdalia hears her grandmother calling. "The movers have taken the last box. We have to go now." Migdalia takes one last look around the bedroom before heading out.

Feelings Feelings Feelings

Ayako saved the most beautifully wrapped present–the one with the big yellow bow and yellow and white striped paper–to open last. She held the box on her lap for just a moment before starting to tear away the paper.

Chantal picked up the phone. "Hi, Dad. Are you leaving your office now? Carrie and I have been ready for ages." "Sorry, hon, maybe later this week. You know I've been working on this big case, and I just can't leave now."

"Everyone said the new baby was so cute, so alert, so this, so that. I don't want to hear any more about the new baby," thought Song.

People sometimes try to hide their feelings from others. But in many cases, letting your feelings show can help you feel better. And when people understand each others' feelings, they find it easier to get along. Think of caring, trusted adults you can approach when you are feeling upset. What qualities do they have that make you feel you can turn to them with personal concerns?

Have you ever seen a public service program on television that offers advice or help to people who have family or emotional problems? Why not create and produce your own? Pick a topic and collect information. Some girls can be on a panel of "experts." Others can be the people with the problems, and one person could be the moderator. You might want to videotape your show for others to view or "take it on the road" for younger girls or other Junior Girl Scout troops or groups.

45

Relating to Boys

Ten-year-old Sonia giggled. She told her best friend Sara about how she watched from the top of the stairs as her older sister and boyfriend kissed on Saturday night. "You know, those long, with-no-time-out-for-breathing kisses," Sonia said

as the school bus took the girls home on Monday afternoon.

"Well, I really like Robert. I can imagine kissing him like that," Sara said quietly, thinking of the cute boy in her fifth-grade class. She watched Sonia's face for her reaction.

Sonia's eyebrows flew right up and her mouth turned into a giant "O." "You'd kiss Robert like that?!"

"S-h-h-h," Sara said. "You don't have to tell the entire bus!"

"I don't think I'm ready for kissing like that, even with Neil, and you know how much I like him."

"I bet Robert and Neil don't think about kissing and touching," Sara said. "Hey, this is my stop—see you tomorrow!"

● ● ● ●

"How was school today, sweetie?" Mom asked Sara. Sara was putting the napkins on the table and started folding one of them into a dog shape–then a cat shape–then a boat. "Sara...?" "Okay, I guess," she answered. She was thinking about her conversation on the bus. She wanted to keep talking but she felt a little embarrassed.

"Is anything wrong, Sara? Did something happen at school?"

"Oh, no," Sara replied. "I was just thinking about something Sonia and I talked about today."

She described the conversation, including the part about the passionate kissing.

"Well, Sara, it's natural to be thinking about boys, but it's just as normal that some girls don't. Everyone develops at her own rate. Some girls your age feel attracted to boys. They want boys to notice them and they want to be close to boys. Other girls just aren't interested at all—and that's okay. Having a crush on a boy is exciting, but it can be kind of scary too. You keep thinking about what he thinks about you!"

"That's it!" Sara said. "You know exactly how I feel."

"When you start going out with a boy–Robert or anyone else–and, by the way, I don't think you're ready to date yet…"

"I knew you would say that…"

"Well, it's true…You learn," her mom continued, "what's it's like to have a special relationship with someone, to have one person to really care about and who really cares about you. Sonia's sister, Dolores, is going out with just one boy now. But last year, Dolores would hang around with a group of boys and girls. They'd go to the movies or to the mall. Group dating is a way to learn about relationships, too. And sometimes, being with a group is easier than being with just one person."

 Talk with friends about the following situations:

1. Sarit finds out the boy she has a crush on doesn't like her.

2. Kim likes Alex. And Alex likes her too. The trouble is Alex has been going with Kim's best friend Suzanne.

WHEN BOYS BOTHER YOU

While it's often nice for you to get attention from boys, sometimes boys say or do things that really bother you. Kwame may think it's cool when he snaps Kendra's bra. Joe may think Tonya should be flattered when he comments about her developing breasts.

Boys, and sometimes girls and grown-ups too, often think that "it's no big deal." But when it's your body someone is talking about or your bra that he is touching, it is a BIG DEAL! You don't have to put up with comments or actions that hurt you or make you feel uncomfortable. In a firm voice, tell anyone who says or does things you don't like to stop.

Turn to page 73 to learn about acting in an assertive way.

If he continues to do things that bother you, or if it is too hard to tell him to stop, tell your parent, teacher, or another grown-up you trust.

WHAT'S IMPORTANT TO

Was it tough answering any of the questions on this page? Your answers show some of your values. Values are those things in which you strongly believe.

Your values influence how you see something, as well as how you react to it. Your dreams, goals, and attitudes are all shaped by your values. If a girl values education, she might not mind having less spending money because she knows her family is saving money for college.

It's important to know what you really value, because those values can help you make decisions. You do this already on a daily basis—how you dress, what your room looks like, how you treat your mom or dad, or even how you relate to your friends—reflect your values.

Values help you use information and decide what you should do. Often, you will need to get more information before making a decision. Suppose you heard your friends arguing about vegetarianism—the belief that people should not eat meat. One of your friends doesn't eat meat because she thinks animals shouldn't be killed. Another friend completely disagrees. She thinks killing animals is okay for food, but she is against hunting as a sport. Another friend thinks killing animals is okay for food, but she is a vegetarian because she thinks it's a healthier way to eat. What do you believe?

How do you decide what to believe and how to act? You are influenced by your family and friends, the media, your community, your spiritual beliefs, and your education.

If you sometimes act in a way that is not in line with what you value, you may feel unhappy. Can you think of a time when you did something that went against what you valued? How did you feel?

• You are getting ready to blast off into outer space to explore the galaxy for one year. What five things would you take with you? Why?

• What do you like most about your best friend? Why?

• What family rule do you feel is most important to keep? Why?

• What if you could choose between having a lovely singing voice or an extremely beautiful face? Which would you pick? Why?

48

YOU?

How important to you are each of these items in the chart below? In Column 1, place a "+" next to those that are very important to you, an "O" next to those that are a little important, and a "–" next to those that are not important.

Values	How I Feel Now Date:	Six Months Later Date:	One Year Later Date:
Being popular at school			
Doing well at school			
Making my own decisions			
Going out with a boy			
Spending time with my family			
Caring for the environment			
Helping others in need			
Standing up for myself			
Exercising and eating good foods			
Wearing expensive clothes			
Fighting prejudice			
Taking part in my religion			
Being with friends			
Other values			

Look at the items you marked as very important. Are you surprised by any of the items you marked? Of the items you marked as very important, which is #1? #2? #3? Place the numbers in the left-hand margin next to the item. Compare your ideas with other girls in your troop or group.

Changes in Values

As you get older, your experiences and the new people you meet may teach you a great deal about yourself and your world, and your values may change. In about six months, reread the values list again, recording your answers in Column 2. What

changes in your values did you find? What are some experiences that caused you to change your values? Are those values that were important before just as important now? Sometime next year, record your answers in Column 3. What changed? What remained the same?

Values in Girl Scouting

Read the lines of both the Girl Scout Promise and Law. The Promise and Law are a set of values shared by all girls who belong to Girl Scouts of the U.S.A. and the World Association of Girl Guides and Girl Scouts.

 With a group of friends, discuss different examples of how you can act on each part of the Girl Scout Law. Discuss how the Girl Scout Promise and Law can be helpful when you are faced with making a tough decision or solving a difficult problem.

Values Dilemmas

Sometimes you are faced with a decision that has no right or wrong answer or you can see both sides of an argument. These choices are called values dilemmas. They can be the hardest decisions you have to make. You may think if you don't act, you are avoiding a choice, but you have made the choice not to act, and that can be worse than not acting at all.

 You have $25 to donate to a local charity. You have thought about making a contribution to a group that provides food to the homeless or to the local animal shelter that is in danger of closing. Who gets the money? Why?

Discuss this dilemma with your group or family. How would you act? Why? What are some of the reasons you decided to act as you did? What are some of the values you used to help make your decision?

 Listed at the right are values that are an important part of Girl Scouting. Look through this book for examples of some of the values.

Keeping traditions

Recognizing the importance of being a girl and a woman

Respecting others

Being honest

Being a good citizen

Giving service to others

Learning about others

Celebrating cultural diversity

Practicing democracy

Recognizing the importance of family

Being a friend

Recognizing the power of an individual

Recognizing the power of group actions

Speaking up for human rights

Believing in yourself

Being a good role model

Working in girl/adult partnerships

Practicing good health and physical fitness

Taking responsibility

Differences in Values

Every day, you will come into contact with people whose values differ from your own. No one should be teased or put down for having different values. And, you have the right to disagree with values different from your own.

 To explore differences in values, try this activity with your friends or family. Think about each statement and decide if you agree, disagree, or are not sure. Explain your feelings and listen carefully to what others say.

• Money brings happiness.

• Women in the military should have combat duty.

• Everyone should have the right to carry a gun.

• Watching violence on television encourages a person to act violently.

Values That Conflict

Sometimes people's values conflict with the rights of others. People who practice racism or discriminate against others hold values that conflict with what our society and the laws of our country value. If you are asked to think seriously about what the United States really stands for, you might think about how the Pledge of Allegiance calls for "liberty and justice for all."

The rights of liberty, justice, and equality are human rights that many people in the United States and throughout the world believe. Although some people may take these rights for granted, the guarantee of these rights has attracted generations of people to the United States like a magnet.

In 1948, long before you were born, the United Nations wrote a Universal Declaration of Human Rights that listed 29 different human rights that were common to people throughout the world.

Some of these rights are listed below. Imagine life without them. Unfortunately, citizens of some countries live without many of these basic rights.

Included in the Universal Declaration of Human Rights are the right to:

✓ Equality

✓ Protection against cruel punishment, like torture

✓ Protection against racial, ethnic, sexual, and religious discrimination

✓ Privacy

✓ Freedom of movement in your country

✓ Seek safety in other countries

✓ Marry whom you want

✓ Own property

✓ Freedom of opinion and speech

✓ Participate in your government

✓ Work and choice of job

✓ Rest and leisure

✓ Education

✓ Know what your rights are

With so many changes in the world, you may have a hard time recognizing when rights are being taken away. Is your mom's right to privacy being violated if someone reads all her computer mail at her place of business? How can you tell if the clothing you buy is being made by children your age being forced to work for pennies in dark, dirty workplaces? Can a boatload of people who claim they are fleeing unfair treatment be turned away? Questions such as these and the way individuals and governments react to them will be important issues in your lifetime.

What's Fair for Girls

Do you get called on in class as often as boys do? Do some adults expect you to have only certain careers when you grow up just because you're a girl? Are the girls and women characters you read about in books or see on television or in the movies strong, successful, and brave? Or are they shown as weak and unable to make decisions? Think about times when you have heard or seen things that did not seem fair to girls. Add your own unfair statements to the cactus on the opposite page.

 To learn more about human rights and the freedoms citizens share, do some activities from badges, such as Active Citizen, Celebrating People, Junior Citizen, World Neighbors, and The World in My Community.

 Interview a person who has lived in another country. What rights were guaranteed there? If possible, speak to someone who came to the United States for a better life.

 Read a newspaper. Look for possible violations of human rights both here and around the world. Share these findings with a group of friends through a discussion, poster, or debate.

HANDBOOK ACTIVITY

Here's a chance for you to see that words can be used to give messages that are fair or unfair. To the right are some examples of statements. With the girls in your troop or group, or on your own, place a "+" next to each statement that sounds fair and a "–" next to each statement that sounds unfair. If you want a real challenge, try changing the unfair statements into fair ones.

___ 1. Hakim Jamal is a smart lawyer and his sister Reza is a pretty redhead.

___ 2. Scientists often become so involved in their work that they forget about their wives and children.

___ 3. Twenty police officers were needed to control the crowd at the baseball stadium.

___ 4. The teacher reminded her students to ask their mothers to send in snacks for the field trip.

___ 5. The candidates were Brendan O'Malley, president of American Electronics, Inc., and Annamarie Piccione, a lively, blonde grandmother of four.

___ 6. The girls took turns throwing the ball.

"Ouch!"

WHAT IS A FAMILY?

Meet seven Junior Girl Scouts—each with a different kind of family*

Stephanie and her older brother live with their dad.

Tatyana is the youngest of five children and lives with her mom and stepdad.

Keisha's family includes her mom, her dad, her older sister, and herself.

Families come in different sizes and forms. You may live with two parents or with one, or you may be cared for and loved by people who are not your parents. You may have many sisters and brothers, two, one, or none. Great-grandparents, grandparents, stepparents, foster parents, guardians, aunts, uncles, and cousins may be part of your family. They may live with you, nearby, or far away. You may see them often or only on special occasions.

Alyssa lives with her mom and grandmother during the week and with her dad and stepmother on the weekend.

54

Locita is the oldest of three children and lives with her dad, her mom, her twin sisters, and her dog.

Lily lives with her mom and her mom's cousin Betty and Betty's daughter.

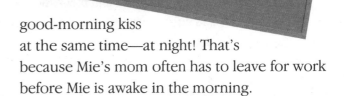

Jennifer lives with her grandmother and pet cat.

HANDBOOK ACTIVITY

Share stories about members of your family or your pets with the girls in your troop or group.

If you have a family photo album, look through it with older members of your family. Ask them to share stories about events that happened in your family when you were young or even before you were born.

Start your own family photo album or scrapbook.

What makes a family special? Family members give each other love and affection. They protect and keep each other safe. They provide food and clothing. You learn all kinds of lessons about growing up from your family. And your family gives you a feeling of belonging and helps you feel good about yourself. These three girls share special nighttime routines with their families.

Before ten-year-old Joanna goes to sleep, her mom always asks her about the best part of her day.

Mie's mom gives her a good-night kiss and a good-morning kiss at the same time—at night! That's because Mie's mom often has to leave for work before Mie is awake in the morning.

Dad used to read aloud to Rika at bedtime, but now that she's nine, Rika reads aloud to Dad—one chapter every night.

What special traditions and celebrations do your family share?

*The names of the girls and the descriptions of their families are made up. They are portrayed here to show the many different types of families girls live in today.

Responsibilities as a Family Member

Members of a family need to work together. Write the chores each member of your family does. Do you see a pattern in who does certain kinds of jobs?

Family Member	Chores
_____	_____
_____	_____
_____	_____
_____	_____
_____	_____

 Some mothers work outside the home for pay and others do not. Talk to at least two women in each group to find out how they manage their responsibilities. Then think about some of the things you juggle in your own life like school, family, and friends. Did you learn anything from talking to the group of mothers that will help you manage your own responsibilities? Discuss what you learned with other girls

 Make a list of some things that girls seem to be expected to do in the home and outside the home. For example, your list might include play with dolls, cook meals, or wear makeup. Make a second list of things that boys seem to be expected to do such as play with trucks, cut the grass, and play basketball. Share your list with others and discuss whether these expectations are unfair and what can be done to change them.

Family Problems

Family life does not always run smoothly. Big and little problems happen in every family. The families you see on television that solve their problems, even very serious ones, in one hour or less are not very realistic. It's important to remember that sometimes, no matter what you do, you have no control over a particular family situation. But, at other times, what you do may help to ease a sticky problem.

Sibling Rivalry

"Stop fighting!" Mrs. Martinez yelled for the third time in two minutes.

"He started it," Tanya explained.

"But she kicked over the building I was making," Eduardo quickly answered.

"It was an accident," Tanya responded.

"It was not. You did it on purpose."

"Did not."

"Yes, you did."

56

Eleven-year-old Tanya and nine-year-old Eduardo, the Martinez children, love each other, but often get into fights. "Sibling rivalry" is what their mother calls it. And she knows that sibling rivalry or arguments between sisters and brothers happen in every family. Whenever people live together, it's natural for arguments to occur.

What kinds of problems happen in families? You do not have to talk about specific examples in your own or another family, but about the types of conflicts that could happen in any family.

 Think of some things you might do to improve communication in your family. Try one of these ideas for at least one week.

Conflict Resolution

One way to solve conflicts (called conflict resolution) is to follow the steps below:

1. Figure out what the problem is.

Every member of the Granger family wants to watch a different television program at 8 o'clock on Tuesday night (and there is only one television).

2. Suggest some solutions to the problem.

Family members could take turns choosing shows. Or the names of the shows could go in a container, and the one selected is the one watched. Or the Grangers might save money to buy a second television.

3. Look at what would happen with each solution.

Choosing a program from a container might result in the same show being watched two or three weeks in a row, and some family members might get angry. The Grangers can't afford to put much money aside right now for a new television. Saving could take more than a year.

4. Make a decision.

After reviewing the suggestions made by all family members and the likely results, the Grangers make a choice. Taking turns selecting the 8 o'clock show on Tuesday night is seen as the best decision by the whole family.

5. Take action.

The Granger family figures out who should make the first selection the following Tuesday night. The plan is put into action.

Teenage Pregnancy

Jessica heard sobs coming from her older sister Nikki's room. Ten-year-old Jessica wanted to share her news about making the soccer team. That would have to wait. "Nikki's probably broken up with her boyfriend–again," thought Jessica. "What's wrong?" Jessica asked. "I could hear you crying even before I got into the house."

"I can't tell you," Nikki answered.

"What do you mean, you can't tell me? You make me tell you everything," Jessica said. "Did something happen to Mom or Dad?" Jessica was really scared now.

"No, no, nothing like that." Nikki cleared her throat and wiped her eyes with a rumpled tissue. She looked down as she said, "I'm pregnant."

Jessica thought, "My intelligent, successful sister–the one who has an A-average, plays the violin in the school orchestra, is the editor of the student newspaper–pregnant. It can't be. She is just 16."

"What?" Jessica asked.

"I'm pregnant," Nikki repeated quietly.

Every year over one million teenage girls get pregnant in the United States. For each of these girls, this one event will forever change her life.

 Learn something about the 24-hour responsibility of motherhood by doing the following activity: Take care of a delicate seedling plant (representing a baby) for at least three days. You will have full responsibility for your "baby," making sure it is always safe, well-fed, and warm. Give your baby four feedings—one teaspoon of water and 1/8 teaspoon of sugar—during the day and night. If you need to leave your baby, even for a short time, you must find a baby-sitter. After the three days, share your experiences. Talk about how your baby changed your daily activities.

Separation & Divorce

Sometimes, conflict between parents is so strong that they divorce or separate. It can be very hard to get used to the idea of living with one parent instead of two. But sometimes it's a relief not to have to listen to the constant fighting between parents, or to be in a home that is very unhappy. Kids in a divorcing family often feel angry with one or both of their parents when divorce happens. Sometimes, they blame themselves, but a parent's leaving is NEVER a child's fault.

Sometimes, family situations change and you may start living with a new stepparent, or grandparent, aunt, or foster family or guardian. Remember that a family is made up of people who care for each other and that as you grow up you may be in more than one type of family situation. Always look for a role model—a strong person who has values you can learn and strengths you can share. A role model will help you get through difficult times—because she or he has taught you how to care for yourself.

A Family Member's Drug or Alcohol Problem

A parent, guardian, or older brother or sister who has a drinking or drug problem is a family problem because it affects every family member. Maybe the person acts very mean or even violently when he or she drinks too much.

Maybe the person is so addicted to drugs that she or he doesn't pay attention to you. What can you do? You should talk about it with other people in your family, a teacher or other trusted adult at school, or a religious or community leader. Find an organization that helps kids from families where drugs and alcohol area problem. There are people who can help you cope with family problems.

A Pet's Death

Felice saw the look on her dad's face. "I have something to tell you, something sad," Dad said. Felice knew what her father was going to tell her, but she wasn't ready to hear the words.

"Spicy's dead." Dad spoke gently as he put his arm around Felice's shoulders.

Tears quickly came to Felice's eyes and spilled down her cheeks. "I know how hard this is for you," Dad said.

"No, you don't," Felice shouted. "Spicy was my dog." She ran to her room sobbing loudly.

Felice's dad knew that she was not really angry with him, but was very upset about the death of her dog. He understood that Felice was feeling sad, angry, even guilty, about Spicy's death, even though it was expected. Spicy had been sick for weeks.

Later on, he and Felice would talk about how Spicy would be buried, and how they would remember her. But right now, Felice just needed to cry.

Have you ever felt sad over the loss of something or someone dear? What helped you get through that sad time?

Perhaps you have a friend who has been touched deeply by a sad family event. You might feel uncomfortable or not know what to say, but a note or a phone call can make a person feel better.

Look in the telephone book for names of agencies that can help people going through difficult times. Create a "Where to Find Help" brochure.

FRIENDS

One of the fun parts of growing up is having friends. Friends make life enjoyable. How would you describe a good friend?

What Kind of Friend Are You?

Think about the kind of friend you are to others. Think about one of your friends. Keep this person in mind as you answer "yes" or "no" to each question below.

	YES	NO
1. I listen carefully to my friend when she talks about something important to her.	___	___
2. When I am upset with my friend I still speak to her.	___	___
3. It doesn't bother me if my friend sometimes has other things to do.	___	___
4. I let my friend know what I like about her.	___	___
5. Sometimes my friend decides how we're going to spend our time together.	___	___
6. My friend and I like to do things together.	___	___
7. I do not try to make my friend be just like me.	___	___
8. I stick up for my friend if I hear others put her down.	___	___
9. I share what I have with my friend.	___	___
10. My friend and I like to do many of the same things.	___	___

Find out what your score means. Count the number of times you said "yes."

If your score is 8–10: You are a super friend!

6–7: You are a very good friend.

4–5: You are a good friend—sometimes.

3 or below: You need to work harder on being a friend.

Make a "Friends" poster. Begin with a slogan that defines what a friend is. Cut out or draw pictures that illustrate friendship or make a list of words that describes a friend. Use these words to design a word puzzle. Have the girls in your troop or group complete the puzzle.

Making Friends

Everybody likes to have friends. But, friendships don't just happen. You have to work at them.

There are no rules about how many friends a person should have. Some girls have many, some a few, and others, only one. Some friends you have throughout life and others come and go as your interests and experiences change.

If you are happy with yourself, you usually find it easier to make and keep friends. Being friendly, upbeat, enthusiastic, and thoughtful are helpful, too. Your Girl Scout troop is a good place to make friends. You can also make friends by joining a club, sports team, or other group at school or in your neighborhood.

 Pretend you are meeting someone for the first time. Think about who that person might be. Tell how you would introduce yourself to her. Talk about what you would say and how you would keep the friendship going. Keep in mind that everyone may not want to be friends. Don't let that stop you from trying to make friends. Always remember that you have a lot to offer.

Make a plan to get to know two people in the next month. Complete the sentences below.

1. Two people I'd like to get to know.

_____   _____

(name of person)   (name of person)

2. Places where I will go to be with them.

_____   _____

_____   _____

3. Things we might talk about.

_____   _____

_____   _____

4. Things we might do together.

_____   _____

_____   _____

Plan a party to celebrate your friendships. Having a party is a great way to get to know people better. You can have a party at home, in a park, in a backyard, at a skating rink, or some other place. A party can be small with just one or two friends, or large with many family members or your Girl Scout group or troop.

Party Planning

Have you ever gone to a party that was a great success? What made it fun? In your Girl Scout troop or group, think of what makes a party fun for the people who are giving the party (hosts) and for people who are attending the party (guests). The chart below will help you plan.

Party Theme _____

_____

Place _____

Guests _____

_____

_____

_____

_____

Food, if any _____

_____

_____

_____

_____

Activities _____

_____

_____

Other _____

_____

_____

Party Popcorn

CAUTION!

Popcorn is an easy party food to make and almost everybody likes it. Here are some recipes to try:

Basic Popcorn

You could buy plain already-popped popcorn, or pop it on the stove following directions on the can, or pop some in the microwave. Make your plain popcorn into party popcorn with these additions:

Cheese Popcorn

Mix 1/2 cup of grated cheese into a large bowl of popcorn.

Cinnamon Sugar

Mix 1/2 cup of plain white sugar with 1 teaspoon of cinnamon and sprinkle over a large bowl of plain popcorn.

Party Activities

If you look through your <u>Junior Girl Scout Handbook</u>, you can find a lot of activities that are fun to do at a party. The activities for practicing your creativity on page 72 could be fun, as could many of the activities in Chapter Seven.

Chocolate Chip Popcorn

Mix 1 cup of small chocolate chips into a large bowl of plain popcorn.

Peanut Pop

Mix a can of roasted peanuts or flavored peanuts into a large bowl of plain popcorn.

Pen Pals

A pen pal is a friend you get to know through letters. She or he usually lives in another state or country, and will write about her or his hometown, school, family, pets, customs and traditions, special interests, or talents. Pen pals share things like games, recipes, solutions to problems, and photos.

Pen Pals Through Girl Scouts of the U.S.A.

Girl Scouts of the U.S.A. provides international pen pal links for Girl Scouts who are ten to seventeen years old. You can request a pen pal by getting a special form from your Girl Scout leader or council. You must use this form to have staff members at national headquarters try to link you with a pen pal in the part of the world you request. (Please send the completed form and a self-addressed stamped envelope; do not send stamps, photographs, or letters about yourself.) Sometimes it isn't possible to find pen pals for everyone. You may reapply after one year if a link is not made.

Peer Pressure

Peers are people in your age group. They may include the girls in your troop or group, your classmates, other friends, and even persons you do not know. Have you ever done or said something because your friends were doing it? Did you do it mainly to keep your friends or to stay a member of the group? That's peer pressure. In a peer pressure situation, everyone is expected to act a certain way, look a certain way, or to have only certain friends.

Peer pressure can be good or bad. It is good when it helps you feel good about yourself and you are learning new skills. Two friends pressured you into presenting your service project idea to your troop. Although you were nervous, your presentation went well and you felt good about all your hard work.

Peer pressure is not so good when it makes you feel uncomfortable, confused, or gets you in trouble. What if your friends convince you to take an unsafe route home?

Why do people pressure others? Some like to control other people. Some think it makes them more popular. Others do it so they can feel important. When faced with peer pressure:

• **Stand up for yourself!** Don't let others lead you to do something you would be ashamed of later.

• **Speak your mind.** Tell people how you really feel. They may learn something new from you.

• **Respect the feelings and decisions of others.** Let others follow their own decisions and you follow yours.

• **Find support from others.** If you feel pressured, talk to someone you trust.

• **Stay away from or ignore the group, if necessary.**

Act out or discuss with a group of friends what you would do in these situations:

•A classmate asks you to cheat on a test.

•Your girlfriend's sister offers you a drink of beer.

•Everyone is wearing designer jeans and your father says it's silly to spend that amount of money on clothes.

•Your stepmother buys you a great outfit. You really like it, but your friends say it is ugly.

•Your parents always expect you to come home early. Your friends make fun of you and call you a baby.

With some friends, put on a skit or play that shows both good and bad types of peer pressure. Write, practice, and perform the play. Invite parents and friends to see the play.

Dear Diary:

I had the most awesome day until just a few minutes ago—Jennifer called! I almost dropped the phone when I heard her voice! I haven't talked to her in weeks because I've been so busy doing things with Mariah and Elizabeth. It's not that I don't like Jennifer anymore, but more like we don't enjoy doing the same things. And Mariah and Elizabeth are so cool—we go shopping together and they love to talk about boys! All Jennifer ever seems to want to do is play video games. Ugh! Now she calls to ask me if I would want to go to the soccer game with her after school tomorrow. I would kind of like to, but I know Elizabeth and Mariah think she's weird—then they'll make fun of me, too! I don't know what to do—maybe I should just make up some excuse to tell Jennifer or go to the game for only a few minutes and hope no one sees me or....

Cliques

Take a look at the top of this page. You might know someone like Stephanie and her friends who make fun of those who look or act differently. This type of group is called a clique. The members of a clique usually share something. For example, the members of a clique may be very good athletes and not friendly to anyone who is not. Some cliques make fun of anyone who is smart or likes school, or of kids who may not be popular.

Members of a clique:

•Leave out kids different from themselves.

•Often tease or make fun of other kids.

•Are hurtful toward other clique members who want out of the clique.

•Aren't open to meeting new people or trying new things.

Read Stephanie's diary at the top of the page. What would you do if you were Stephanie? On the diary page (see next page), write what you would say to Jennifer. When you are finished, share your thoughts with others.

65

Gangs

The word "gang" can be used to describe a group of friends who enjoy spending time together. However, when activities that are illegal are involved, the word "gang" takes on a very different meaning. This kind of gang controls the kids who are its members, forcing them to do things that are often violent and criminal.

Gangs can be found in large cities, small towns, and suburban and rural areas. How do you know if a gang has formed in your community? Many gangs use or wear specific colors or symbols, and make all gang members agree to follow special rules. Many gangs use graffiti to mark an area as their own. Gangs also send out threats against other groups in the community, and, when a violent act has occurred, let others know they were responsible. Talk about gangs with members of your troop or group. Discuss the following:

• Why do kids join gangs? What do they get from gangs that they can't get from their families and communities?

• What are some things kids can do instead of joining gangs? How can a community help prevent kids from joining gangs?

• What are three things you would say to a kid who is in a gang?

Bullies

Every afternoon for the last two weeks, Damaris has followed Michelle home from school. Damaris calls her names, tries to get her to fight, and takes money from her. Michelle is afraid to tell her grandmother because she doesn't want Damaris to find out she told someone.

Damaris is a bully. If you have not already come into contact with a bully, sooner or later you will. Bullies usually shove, punch, steal from, make fun of, fight, or pick on others. Bullies are usually people who feel hurt, angry, afraid, or frustrated inside, and they take it out on others.

Write to Stephanie Here

_____

_____

_____

_____

_____

_____

_____

_____

_____

_____

_____

_____

_____

_____

_____

With a group of friends talk about ways you have been bullied. Discuss ideas on how to handle a bully.

Have you ever bullied others? Do you know why you acted like a bully? Do you know how to stop?

To handle a bully you might: stand up for yourself, ignore her, walk away, refuse to fight, talk it out, scream or yell, or get help from an adult. Turn to pages 46–48 for ideas on handling conflicts and being assertive. Share this information with someone you know who is being bullied. Remember, a bully has no right to hurt you or anyone else.

Peer Support

Your peers can be a source of support for you. You can grow together, learn more about yourself and each other, and do activities. You can share skills, study hard, and achieve goals together. To help you decide whether a group of friends are right for you, ask yourself these questions:

• Do I feel comfortable?

• Do they accept me for who I am?

• Are their values the same as mine?

• What do they expect of me?

• Do they make me happy or angry most of the time?

• Do they make me feel good or bad about myself?

• Do I want others to know I'm part of this group?

If you have answered yes to most of these questions, this peer group is probably right for you.

Adults

You spend a lot of time with people your own age, but many adults are also part of your life. Your life is certainly influenced by the adults around you–family members, teachers, religious leaders, your Girl Scout leader, and your friends' parents. There may be some adults who understand you better than others. You may have a great time with some adults and not get along with others. That's a part of growing up.

 Make a list of the most important adults in your life. Write down their names and tell why they are important to you.

 Do or make something for a special adult. Write a letter, make a gift, or surprise her or him with a phone call.

Making Decisions and Solving Problems

Remember the section on values earlier in this chapter? It was mentioned that values influence decisions you make. In the following decision-making story maze, you get to be the main character. Follow the story wherever it leads you and see what choices you make. You might want to read the sections "Making Good Decisions," "Communication," and "Creative Solutions" when you're done with the story maze. Mark a ● where good decision-making is needed. Mark a ▲ where communication is needed. Mark a ■ where creative problem-solving is needed.

You and your best friend Monique are on your way home from school. Up ahead, you see the new girl in your class, Tina, walking alone. Monique tells Tina to wait; the three of you start walking together. Tina invites you and Monique to her house for a snack. Monique thinks it's a good idea and decides to go. You know that you have to go straight to your neighbor's house from school. Your mother doesn't think you are old enough to stay alone for an hour and a half. This makes you feel like a baby, and you always try to get her to change her mind. Now you have a chance to do something more grown up. What do you do? If you say "I can't, I have to go home right after school," go to **A.** If you say, "Sure, but only for a little while," go to **B.**

A. You cross the street and continue on your way. When you reach your neighbor's home, no one is there. You ring the doorbell several times. Still, there is no answer. You think this is very odd. Something very important must have happened for her to not be there. If you go into the backyard to do your homework and wait, go to **C.** If you try to catch up with Tina and Monique, go to **H.**

B. When you get to Tina's house, there are no adults at home, but her teenage brother and his two friends are there. You know your parents don't want you visiting a friend when there are no adults present. You tell Monique that you think you should leave. Just then Tina's brother offers to let you girls tag along with his friends to the mall. Everyone thinks it's a good idea. If you go to the mall with the others, go to **D.** If you say "Good-bye" and go on to your neighbor's home, go to **E.**

C. You've just finished your math assignment when your neighbor comes into the backyard. "I'm so glad you waited for me," she says. "I was stuck in the worst traffic jam. I knew you were responsible and would wait for me."
THE END.

Communication

Communication is the ability to express your thoughts, feelings, and beliefs. Good communication skills are important in decision-making and problem-solving. Communicating well is a skill that takes practice. There are two types of communication—verbal and nonverbal. Using words to say what you mean is verbal communication. Using symbols, signs, or body language is nonverbal communication.

When people speak, they want others to hear and understand what they are saying. Here are tips for being a good listener.

- Pay attention to the person who is talking. Make eye contact.
- Concentrate on what the other person is saying.
- Try not to interrupt or think about how you will answer.
- Ask questions to help you understand what you heard.
- Repeat in your own words what you heard the person say when she or he is finished speaking.

How do you rate as a listener?

Making Good Decisions

When making a tough decision, it sometimes helps to follow a step-by-step process. Using the steps below may help you determine the best choice. You may not always need every step except to make big decisions.

1. Figure out the problem or issue.
2. Collect information about yourself and the situation—think about your values, goals, and interests.
3. Think of as many solutions to the problem as you possibly can.
4. Look at the good points and bad points (pros and cons) of each solution.
5. Make a decision.
6. Take action.
7. Evaluate: Are you happy with the decision you made?

Think about a tough decision you recently made. How might these steps have helped you? Try using these steps to help with your next decision.

D. You all pile into Tina's brother's car and go to the mall. When you get there the teenagers decide to go off by themselves. They will meet you in an hour. Tina, Monique, and you decide to look in a music store. Tina and Monique go down one aisle. You see a CD that you heard in a movie and go down that aisle. The next thing you know, Tina and Monique are gone. You think that maybe they are playing a trick on you and hiding. You look all over the store. You can't find them. You ask the cashier if she saw your friends. She says she thinks she saw them leave. If you go to the information booth and have them paged, go to **F.** If you call your father who works nearby to pick you up, go to **G.**

E. When you reach your neighbor's house, she says that she was just about to get worried. She expected you home sooner, and was just about to call the school. You apologize and start doing your homework.
THE END.

F. Tina's brother and his friends meet you at the information booth. So do Tina and Monique. They apologize for playing that mean trick on you and decide to leave the mall. They drop you off at your neighbor's home. When you get there, she is very upset with you for being late. She promises to tell your parents when they get home.

THE END.

G. Your father tells you to stay where you are and he'll be right there. On the way home, he tells you that you should have known better than to get in a car with strangers or people you don't know well. You tell him that you thought you would be safe. He continues to talk about all of the horrible things that could have happened to you, and now you will be grounded for a month.

THE END.

H. You run to the corner where you left Monique and Tina. You see no sign of them. You don't know where Tina lives, so you head back to your neighbor's house. On your way, you decide to take a shortcut through the park. You see a group of older kids who are smoking. You recognize one of them. She calls you over and introduces you to her friends. They ask if you would like a cigarette. If you decide to take one, go to **I**. If you say "No thanks!" and walk away, go to **J**.

Creative Solutions

To solve problems creatively, keep your mind open. If you do not solve a problem one way, try a different way. If that doesn't work, find a third way.

To get better at creative problem-solving:

- Practice your creativity. List different ways to use a piece of plain white paper (not just as a surface for writing). For example, you can make a paper airplane, wrap a present, make confetti, use as a mask, or crush into a ball. Do the same with a cup, a pencil, a sock. Think of other examples. The more you practice, the more creative you will become.

- Brainstorm with a group. You can often come up with creative solutions by listening to the ideas of others.

- Take a break from problem-solving to solve problems! When concentrating on a problem doesn't work, a change of scenery or activity may be helpful. You may find that when you are resting or playing with friends, an answer to a problem will suddenly appear.

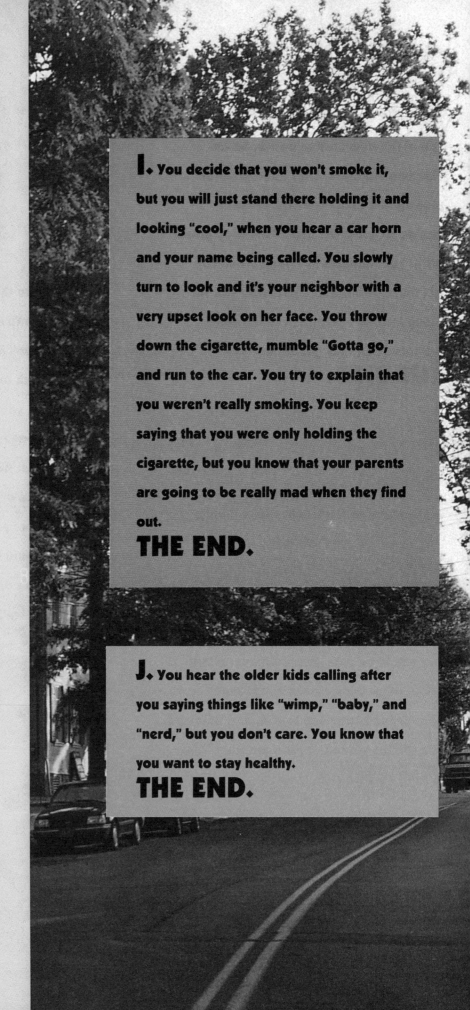

I. You decide that you won't smoke it, but you will just stand there holding it and looking "cool," when you hear a car horn and your name being called. You slowly turn to look and it's your neighbor with a very upset look on her face. You throw down the cigarette, mumble "Gotta go," and run to the car. You try to explain that you weren't really smoking. You keep saying that you were only holding the cigarette, but you know that your parents are going to be really mad when they find out.

THE END.

J. You hear the older kids calling after you saying things like "wimp," "baby," and "nerd," but you don't care. You know that you want to stay healthy.

THE END.

You respond to conflict or difficult situations in different ways. Your response may be different depending on whom you are talking to (friends, teachers, parents, sisters or brothers) or what the issue is.

Suppose you and your friends are trying to decide on a movie. One person suggests going to see a horror movie and the others all start agreeing. But, you hate horror movies. To respond **assertively**, you say, "I really hate horror movies. How about seeing *Jet Pilot III* with Tom News? He's great! Or, I heard *Superwoman* is really good—and it's playing right down the street." You've let your friends know that you would prefer to see another movie and you've given the group a couple of choices.

If you responded **aggressively**, you could have said, "I'm Not Going to THAT Movie and I'm Going to Just Sit Right Here until you all come up with a better idea!" You also have let people know that you want to see another movie, but you've made it difficult for them to respond to you in a positive way.

What if you just went along with the others and didn't say anything at all because you were afraid to speak up? That would be a **passive** response. A passive response means you have made the choice not to make a choice or a decision. You are letting others make choices for you.

Assertiveness involves expressing yourself honestly, standing up for yourself, and showing respect for the rights and feelings of others. When you communicate in an aggressive way, you use harsh words, maybe some hurtful ones, to express yourself. While an assertive way of speaking and acting is almost always better, sometimes an aggressive response may be appropriate. What if you have told someone twice already to stop tickling you so hard?

Learn about body language by watching people. Observe three people (children or adults) at home, at play and at work or school. Watch how they sit, stand, gesture, and move. Discuss what you have observed at a troop or group meeting.

Read the situations below and decide which would be the best way to respond. Maybe you could act them out showing different ways of responding.

• You have been waiting on line 30 minutes to purchase tickets to a movie. An announcement is made that there are only 20 tickets left. Suddenly, a boy your age jumps in line ahead of you. This may prevent you from getting a ticket.

• Your mom tells you to clean up your room. You are supposed to be at your friend's apartment in five minutes and your sister was the one who made the mess.

• One of the girls in your class—a really big bully—takes your pencil off your desk for the

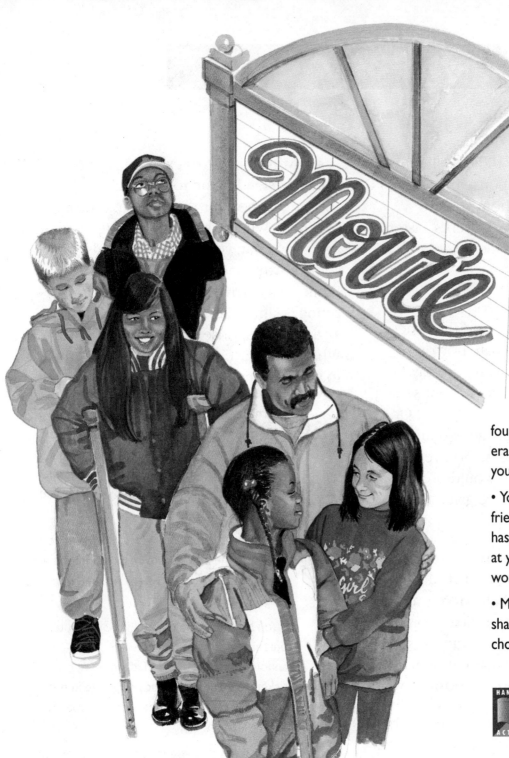

fourth time today—chews the eraser and then throws it back to you.

• You are sleeping over at your friend's house and her grandmother has made dinner for you. You look at your plate—fish sticks—your worst nightmare food.

• Make up your own situations or share a time when you had to choose how to respond.

 Look at items F, I, and J in the decision-making story maze and decide which responses are passive, assertive, and aggressive.

If you still have questions now that you have finished this chapter, ask your parent or guardian. Remember, no question is ever too silly or unimportant.

STAYING SAFE AND HEALTHY

Taking care of yourself means guarding your safety, caring for your body, and eating right. Ahead in this chapter, you'll find lots of tips, facts, and activities on such things as first aid, personal safety, body care, and healthy food. See if you can come up with your own ideas for safety and health activities to share with your troop or group.

Safety Do's and Don'ts
page 76

Try a New Hairstyle
page 88

Rules to Eat by
page 95

When Stress Becomes Unmanageable
page 91

Staying Safe

Whether you're home, at the park, at a friend's house, or walking down the street, you need to know safety skills.

CAUTION!

SAFETY DO'S AND DON'TS

SAFETY TIPS FOR TRAVEL

DO obey traffic signals and signs. Also, obey traffic police, crossing guards, and student safety patrols.

DO look both ways before you cross.

DO walk where you can see and be seen by other people.

DO follow the buddy system. When you are with someone else, you can look after each other.

DO go immediately to a police officer, an adult you know, or into a store if you think someone is following you.

DO wear seat belts when riding in a car, even if the trip is short.

DO wear light or white clothing when walking at dusk or night.

DO sit in a place on a bus or train where the conductor or driver can see you. If another passenger is bothering you or making you feel uncomfortable, tell the driver or conductor.

DO have your house key ready–but hidden from the sight of others–so you can go right into your house or apartment.

DO carry extra change in case you need to make an emergency call. **DO** keep your wallet or money in a front pocket. **DO** carry your purse under your arm (like a football) or wear it with the strap across your body.

DO know where to get help, how to do basic first aid, and what to do if you accidentally get separated from a group.

DON'T walk in the roadway, on the curb, or between parked cars.

DON'T take shortcuts through dark alleys, vacant lots, or abandoned buildings.

DON'T leave your buddy or your group.

DON'T take candy, gum, money, or other gifts from a stranger.

DON'T distract the driver, fool around, or stick your head or hands out a window when riding in a car or bus.

DON'T walk alone when it is dark.

DON'T enter your house or apartment if you think a stranger is inside. Go to a neighbor for help.

DON'T play on an elevator.

SAFETY TIPS FOR PUBLIC SPACES

DO go immediately to a police officer, an adult you know, or into a store if you think someone is following you.

DO pick a meeting place beforehand in case you're separated from family or friends.

DO remain calm if you get lost.

DON'T be afraid to scream or yell if someone tries to get you to leave with him or her.

DON'T wander off alone.

DON'T play in deserted or out-of-the-way places, such as alleys and dead-end streets.

DON'T play around construction sites, abandoned buildings, or in vacant lots.

SAFETY TIPS FOR WEATHER

DO seek shelter during a storm. Stay away from tall objects like trees and poles. If you can't get inside, look for a low place and crouch down as low as you can. Lightning will often strike the highest point in an area. In a flat, open field that could be you.

DO be careful after a storm. Stay away from downed power lines (they may still be electrified and could shock you); loose tree branches (they could fall); deep puddles (they may be full of pollution, could carry an electric shock, or could be deeper than you think).

DO turn off the television and other electrical appliances if lightning occurs. Close windows. Try not to use the telephone. If you must use the telephone during a storm and you hear crackling noises on the line, hang up immediately. Lightning can travel along a phone line and shock you.

DO make sure you have emergency supplies at home. Make a regular check of your supplies. You should have a flashlight, extra batteries, a battery-powered radio, an emergency supply of candles, small cans of cooking fuel or a camp stove, a supply of water, and ingredients for making a meal that requires no cooking or water.

DO stay out of ditches and arroyos as flash floods could be heading your way.

DO go to the basement or the lowest point of a building if a tornado is heading your way.

DO dress properly. Being too hot or too cold can be harmful.

DO protect yourself against sunburn. Use sunscreen.

DON'T ignore your body's warning signals. Shivering is an early sign of hypothermia—too little body heat. Dizziness, weakness, and nausea are early warning signs of hyperthermia—too much body heat.

First-Aid

First aid is the care you give someone who is hurt or ill before medical help arrives. Knowing first-aid skills and safety rules can help prevent accidents and prepare you for an emergency.

FIRST-AID KIT

Having a first-aid kit on hand and knowing how to use it can help you be prepared. With your troop or group or family, put together a first-aid kit. Here are some items to include:

- First-aid book
- Soap
- Safety pins
- Scissors
- Distilled water (in an unbreakable container)
- Tweezers
- Sewing needle to remove splinters
- Matches
- Adhesive tape and bandages
- Flashlight
- Paper drinking cups
- Sterile gauze
- Triangular bandage or clean cloth
- Cotton swabs
- Oral thermometer
- Latex gloves
- Instant chemical ice pack
- Pocket face-shield
- Plastic bag
- Emergency telephone numbers
- Change for telephone call

When an accident or emergency happens, stay calm and, if possible, get an adult to help you.

If the injury is serious, call a doctor right away. Do not move an injured person unless there is danger like a fire or exposed electrical wires. Always tell an adult afterwards if you have given someone first aid. Wear latex gloves to protect yourself from blood or other bodily fluids.

First-Aid Guide

Animal Bite

Wash the wound with soap and warm water. Apply a sterile bandage or cloth. Call a doctor or hospital. Try to identify the animal in case it needs to be tested for rabies.

Bleeding

•*Small cuts*: Latex gloves must be worn when caring for bleeding wounds. Clean the cut with soap and warm water, and cover with a bandage.

•*Large wounds that will not stop bleeding*: Rest a clean cloth directly on the wound and press firmly. Apply pressure until the bleeding stops. Use adhesive tape to hold the cloth in place. Raise the bleeding part above the level of the person's heart if possible. Call a doctor.

Blisters

Wash the area with soap and warm water. Cover with a clean bandage. Do not break the blister.

Bumps and Bruises

Put a cold, damp cloth on the area. If there is a lot of swelling, call an adult for help.

Burns

If the burn has not broken or charred the skin, rest the burned area in cold (not ice) water, pat dry, and cover with a dry, sterile cloth. Do not use ointment, butter, or petroleum jelly. Have an adult check the burn. Call a doctor or the hospital if the skin is broken, blistered, or charred.

Choking

If the person can speak, cough, or breathe, do nothing. Otherwise, stand behind the person and grasp your hands around her, just under her rib cage. Press your hands into her stomach with four quick upward moves. Do this until the person spits out the stuck food or object.

Drowning

Someone should call the lifeguard or go for help immediately. It's important to get the person out of the water. Try to cover the mouth and nose with thin material or the face mask from your first-aid kit and find an adult to do CPR and rescue breathing. Then follow the directions for treating hypothermia.

Eye Injuries

When a person gets hit in the eye, put a cold, clean cloth over it. Have the eye checked by a doctor.

• *Foreign objects*: If small objects (like an eyelash or piece of dirt) get into the eye, do not allow the person to rub her eye. Use a cup filled with cool water to rinse the eye. (Do this over a sink, if possible.) Have the person bend so that her head is sideways. Pour water over the opened eye, and tell the person to move her eyeball up and down. If an object is sticking into the eyeball, do not attempt to remove it. Call a doctor or hospital immediately.

• *Chemical burns*: If bleach or some other cleaning chemical gets into the eye, immediately rinse it with cool water from a running faucet or cup for at least 15 minutes. To rinse, turn the person's head to the side so that the eye with the chemical burn is on the bottom. Let water run slowly across the eye starting from the part closest to the nose. Cover the eye with a clean, dry cloth. Call a doctor or hospital immediately.

Fainting

Help the person lie down or bend over with her head between her knees. Loosen tight clothing. Wipe her face with cool water. Call a doctor if the person doesn't open her eyes quickly.

Fractures, Sprains, Broken Bones

Do not move the injured person. Keep the person calm. Call a doctor or hospital.

Frostbite

Frostbite occurs when part of the body starts to freeze. The skin turns white, grayish yellow, or pale blue. As quickly as possible, warm the area. Put the frozen area into warm (not hot) water. Dry very gently (do not rub or press hard) and wrap in warm cloth, blankets, or both. Call a doctor.

Hyperthermia (too much body heat)

Heat exhaustion is mild; heat stroke is severe. Get the person out of the sun and cool her off. Have her slowly drink cool (not cold) water. Call a doctor if the person is very hot, not sweating, pale, nauseous, has trouble breathing, and seems dazed.

Hypothermia (too little body heat)

Get the person out of the cold, and warm her body slowly. Remove wet clothing and cover with dry clothing or blankets. If person is conscious and able to swallow, give warm liquids. Call a doctor or hospital.

Insect Stings and Tick Bites

Remove the stinger if you can. Don't use tweezers, as this may cause poison to be pumped into the bitten area. Instead, scrape across the top of the skin. Wash the area with soap and water, and apply ice to reduce the swelling. If there is a lot of swelling, or if the person seems to be getting sick or showing signs of shock, there may be an allergic reaction. In this case, call a doctor or hospital immediately.

• *Tick bite*: Use tweezers to pull the tick out directly. Put the tweezers as close to the tick's head as possible. Save the tick. (Tape it onto a white piece of paper.) Your doctor can test it for Lyme and other diseases.

Nosebleed

Have the person sit forward on a chair with her head bent slightly forward. Pinch the lower part of her nose for at least five minutes to stop the bleeding. Then place a cold, wet cloth on her nose and face.

Poisoning

Call your local poison control center or a doctor for help immediately. To prevent poisoning, look through your home for things that might be poisonous, such as medicines, cleaning fluids, plants, and cosmetics. With the help of an adult, label all poisons and store them in a safe place—out of the reach of young children.

Shock (can occur in any kind of emergency)

You may notice sweating, rapid breathing, nausea, and cold or clammy skin. Keep the person lying down. Elevate the feet. Place one cloth or blanket under the person and another cloth or blanket over her. Try to keep her comfortable and calm. Call a doctor.

Snakebite

If you cannot be sure that the snake was not poisonous, treat the snakebite like a poisonous one. Calm the person. Keeping a person calm makes her blood, and the poison, move more slowly. Get her to a doctor or hospital as soon as possible. If you can, carry her because you do not want the poison to circulate too quickly.

Splinter

Gently wash the area with clean water. Look for the edge of the splinter and try to pull it out using your fingertips or tweezers. Be careful not to push the splinter under the skin.

Sunburn

Prevent sunburn by using sunscreens. Look for lotions or creams with an SPF (Sun Protection Factor) number of 15 or higher. Limit your time in the sun and remember that sunburns can happen on hazy, cloudy days too. If a sunburn occurs, gently soak the burned area in cold water. Do not put ice on the area. If the person is in a great deal of pain, call a doctor.

Emergency Telephone Calling

Practice making some emergency telephone calls in your troop or group or with an adult. Learn how to give the most important information quickly and how to follow the directions given to you. Here are some practice situations. Try making up your own.

- You smell smoke in the hallway of your apartment building.
- Your friend accidentally drank some kerosene that was stored in a soda bottle.
- You are home alone and you hear glass breaking downstairs.
- The lights suddenly go out in the house.

Keep an up-to-date emergency telephone number list near every phone in your home.

EMERGENCY TELEPHONE LIST

Mom (or guardian) at work: _____

Dad (or guardian) at work: _____

Parents'/guardians' home phone numbers: _____

Other relatives: _____

Neighbors: _____

Emergency medical services: _____

Police: _____

Fire department: _____

Poison control center: _____

Doctor: _____

Dentist: _____

Utilities: _____

Taxi or car service: _____

Other important numbers: _____

_____

_____

Fire Safety

One way to practice fire safety is to prevent fires from starting. Check your home, the place where you meet for Girl Scouts, or other places for fire hazards.

 Try to come up with a list of fire hazards. You can do this by yourself, with one or two friends, or in your Girl Scout troop or group. (Turn the page upside down to see a list. How many did you know?)

FIRE HAZARDS

- Electrical outlets with too many plugs
- Frayed electrical cords
- Portable heaters near curtains, fabric chairs and sofas, or beds
- Paint and cleaning supplies stored in places that can get hot
- Newspapers stacked in large piles
- Appliances plugged into extension cords for a long time
- Paint-stained, dirty, or oily rags piled together
- Curtains or towels hanging close to a stove or oven
- Full ashtrays
- Vases full of water placed on a television or other electrical appliance
- Matches or lighters left within the reach of young children
- Electrical appliances plugged in near sinks and bathtubs
- Pot handles sticking over stove tops
- Towels and other cloths used as pot holders

SOME FIRE-SAFETY RULES

If fire breaks out at home, remember these rules:

1. Get yourself and others out of the house quickly. Do not go back for anything or anyone.

2. Don't stay and try to put out the fire. Fires spread very quickly.

3. Call the fire department from outside. Give your name and address and the exact place of the fire. If you use a fire alarm box, stay near it so you can direct the fire truck once it arrives.

If smoke comes into a room and the door is closed:

1. Do not open the door.

2. Feel the door. If it is cool, open it a little and hold it with your foot. Feel the air outside with your hand. If the air is not hot, walk outside immediately. Use fire stairs, not elevators. If the door is warm, block the crack under the door with pillows, sheets, blankets, or a rug. Go to the window and call for help. Stay near the window until help arrives. Cover your nose and mouth with a wet cloth, if possible, and wet the materials you are using to block the door.

If you wake up and the room is full of smoke:

1. Roll out of the bed directly onto the floor.

2. Crawl to the nearest exit. Smoke rises, so the coolest, freshest air will be close to the floor. Remember not to open any door without first checking to see if it is warm.

If fire breaks out when you are in a public place:

1. Stay calm.

2. Walk quickly and quietly to the nearest exit.

An important fire-safety skill is to note the fire exits or the quickest way to leave whenever you are in a public space.

Stop, Drop, and Roll

Look at these illustrations. They demonstrate STOP–DROP–ROLL—the technique to use if your or another person's clothes catch on fire.

If your clothes catch on fire:

1. **STOP**–where you are.

2. **DROP**–to the floor or ground. Do not run. Running feeds more oxygen to the fire and makes it burn faster.

3. **ROLL**–back and forth making sure to cover your face with your hands. Or wrap a coat, blanket, or rug around you to smother the flames.

If another person's clothes are on fire:

1. Get the person to **STOP**

2. Get the person to **DROP** to the ground.

3. **ROLL** the person over and over or wrap a blanket, coat, or rug around her to smother the flames.

 Find out how a smoke detector works and where to place one in an apartment, house, troop meeting place, or other location.

Plan and practice fire escape routes. Draw a fire escape plan for the place where you live, your troop or group meeting place, or school. Be sure to include at least two ways to escape.

Invite a firefighter to visit and speak to your troop or group.

Design a safety knowledge test for your group. Try to make it a game, a skit, or a relay race.

Personal Safety

Personal safety means protecting yourself from physical harm caused by other people. People you know and people you don't know can hurt you. You can learn how to protect yourself from abuse–treatment that is injuring or harmful–and how to tell someone you trust if you have been abused.

Sexual harassment is a form of abuse in which someone says things or touches you in ways you do not want or in ways that make you uncomfortable. Sexual harassment is also when someone asks you to do sexual things you do not want to do. Usually the person who is doing the harassing feels that he or she can make the person being harassed feel afraid. Tell the person harassing you to stop it. Another way to stop sexual harassment is to tell someone you trust. If the person you tell doesn't believe you, tell someone else.

Sexual abuse is when an adult or child touches you in a way that makes you uncomfortable or that hurts you, and when the reason for the touching is to make the child or adult feel good. Sexual abuse can happen within a family or with someone you know well. This is a very difficult situation for kids because sometimes they believe that the abuse is their fault or they feel something terrible will happen if they tell. Abuse is wrong. If someone tries to abuse you, it is absolutely your right to say "NO!" You should tell

PERSONAL SAFETY DO'S AND DON'TS

When You're Out and About

DON'T play in deserted areas or out-of-the-way places, like alleys, dead-end streets, construction sites, empty laundry rooms, abandoned buildings, rooftops and elevators, train tracks, truck yards, quarries, or vacant lots.

DO scream or yell if someone tries to get you to go with him or her. You can yell "Fire" or "Help–this person is not my parent," or "Help–I don't know this person."

DO go to a police station, store salesperson, or a uniformed official if you feel you are being followed or if something makes you nervous.

DON'T believe a message a stranger gives you like, "Your mother wants me to bring you home."

When You're Home Alone

DON'T open the door to a stranger, even if he or she is in uniform and has a package or flowers to deliver. Either tell the person to come back another time or just don't answer the door.

DO keep all doors and windows locked.

DO know how to answer the phone when you are home alone. Practice answering the phone in your Girl Scout troop or group or with family members.

DON'T give a person who calls the "wrong" number your telephone number, even if he or she insists. Just say, "You have the wrong number" and hang up.

DO call the police or your emergency assistance number if you hear or see someone trying to break into your home.

an adult you trust, and if this adult does not believe you, tell another trusted adult.

If you have been abused, tell someone. If you know someone who is being abused, get her to tell. Most communities have abuse hotlines to call, or you can call the police.

You can learn to protect yourself by avoiding potentially dangerous situations. However, if someone does harm you, try to remember: When did it happen? Where did it happen? What happened? Who was there? What did the person (or persons) look like? If the person was in a car, what did the car look like? Can you remember the license plate number?

Personal Safety Role-Playing

What would you do in these situations?

•You and your cousins are playing outside. Your older cousin starts tickling you so hard that it hurts.

•You wake up in the night when someone you know is sitting on your bed and touching you in places that make you feel uncomfortable.

•One of the older boys in the neighborhood asks if you want to play "special grown-up games" with him. He says you have to promise not to tell.

•You are at the shopping mall with your grandmother when you see this great pair of shoes in a store window. You run over to look. When you turn around, you can't see your grandmother.

•You are at the movies with friends. A man sits next to you and accidentally brushes your leg and says, "Sorry." When the movie starts, he does it again.

TRY THESE SAFETY ACTIVITIES:

 In your troop or group, brainstorm safety situations that fit into the categories of weather, water, personal safety, fire, and emergency preparedness. Role-play safe ways to act in these situations.

 Read the decision-making story maze on pages 68–71. A lot of the choices involve staying safe. Create your own safety story or safety skit that has different endings depending upon the path you choose.

 Create a game on safety using the information in this chapter. It could be a card game, board game, or a wide game (a game in which you move from station to station).

 Find out about bicycle safety and show that you know how to inspect and safely ride a bicycle.

 Pick a sport and create a safety checklist, poster, or booklet for that sport. (See pages 147–150 for sports ideas.)

STAYING HEALTHY

Taking Care of Your Body

Do you ever think about how you look? Do you wonder what other people think about how you look? Though people should judge others by what's on the inside–qualities like kindness and a good sense of humor, for example–lots of times a first impression is made by one's appearance. Keeping your body and clothing clean are some ways you show others that you care about yourself. The healthy habits you form now will help you be a healthy adult.

Your Skin

Sweat glands might make you perspire a lot during puberty. Sometimes, your skin gets oilier and, if you feel nervous or worried, you may start to sweat heavily. If this sweat is left on the body too long, bacteria will cause it to have an

odor. You may need to use a deodorant or antiperspirant daily.

It is important to wash every day. Set a time to bathe or shower regularly and, if you exercise, you may want to bathe again.

Always wash your hands after you have used the bathroom, before you eat, and before and after you have handled food. Unclean hands can spread disease.

Cleanliness is especially important during menstruation because the hormones (chemicals made by glands in your body) that control your period also cause sweat glands to be more active. At that time of the month, your skin and hair may be oilier.

When You're in the Sun

Protecting your skin from the sun is important. Even on cloudy or cold days, ultraviolet rays from the sun can damage your skin. You won't see the damage right away, but you will when you are older–wrinkles, lines, and maybe even skin cancer. Sunscreens come in different degrees of protection. A rating of 15 or higher should protect your skin, but you need to apply it before you go out into the sun and after swimming or exercise.

Your Face

Washing your face not only keeps you looking clean, but rids your skin of extra oil, dirt, and bacteria that can cause pimples.

Almost everyone gets pimples at some time or another. When girls and boys enter puberty, they may find their skin becoming oily, and they may get pimples and blackheads. Acne is a skin disease in which the oil glands in your skin get swollen and blocked causing pimples and blackheads. A dermatologist has medicines and tips that can help control acne. Keep hair and hands off your face, and don't pick or squeeze pimples. You can scar your face!

Teeth

When you smile, you want people to notice your clean, healthy teeth.

To keep teeth healthy, remember these tips:

* Remove plaque (a combination of saliva, bacteria, and food particles) often. Plaque can cause cavities if it remains on your teeth, and it can cause bad breath.

* Brush after meals and use dental floss, because a toothbrush can't clean between your teeth.

* Eat raw fruits and vegetables, like apples, carrots, and celery.

Good dental habits are especially important if you wear braces as food can get stuck in the wires or bands.

Your Hair

Wash, shampoo, and condition your hair regularly. How often to wash depends on your hair type.

Some girls wash their hair once a week and some once a day. When it comes to hair care products—creams, mousses, curl activators, gels, sprays, relaxers, and permanents— choose those that are best for your hair type. Remember, all products have the potential to damage hair if misused or overused. This is also true of blow dryers, hot combs, and curling irons. So be careful and check with your parent or guardian.

HAIRSTYLES

Changing your hairstyle can give you a new look. Try bangs; part your hair differently; braid it; put ornaments in it. Below are different ways to braid hair. Remember, the best hairstyle for you is the one you like the most. You might feel pressured to have the same hairstyle as a friend or want to look like a performer you admire. But you have to decide if that hairstyle works with your type of hair and the shape of your face.

French Braids

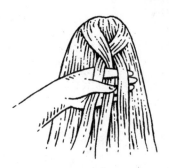 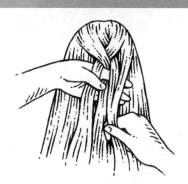 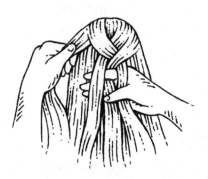

1. Divide the hair at the top of the head into three sections.

2. Cross the right and then the left section over the center section.

3. Take a small section of hair from the right side of the face. Add this hair to the right section of the braid.

4. Pull the center section all the way to the right.

5. Hold all of the braid in your right hand and then repeat the process on the left side.

6. Continue moving from the right to the left until all the hair on either side has been caught up in the braid. Finish by braiding the bottom or turning the hair under into a roll.

Corn Row Braids

1. Divide a section of hair into a straight row.

2. Start making a tight braid adding hair from the right and the left and pulling to keep the braid neat and tight as you did with the French Braid, but using smaller amounts of hair within the two straight sides of the row.

3. Once you have braided all the hair in the row, secure the ends, if needed, with a band, clip, or bead.

4. You can make more intricate patterns by braiding in circles or swirls.

Why not hold a braid workshop or fashion show for other Girl Scout troops or groups?

Create your own party barrettes or fashion barrettes and bows to match different outfits. Braid into your hair beads and ribbons. Take a plain headband and wrap it with ribbons, fabric, or yarn. Sew or glue on beads or bows.

Have a hairstyle party. Use the ideas here or look through magazines, talk with older girls or adults, or dream up some new hair creations! Try different hairstyles on each other. To keep things clean, it's best not to share brushes, combs, and other hair appliances that touch the hair. If you can, take some instant pictures or find another way to keep a record of your new looks!

Create a "Looking Your Best" booklet, poster, video, or collage. Look through Chapter Two for some ideas about the images of beauty. These badges, in *Girl Scout Badges and Signs*, may also help: Becoming a Teen, Health and Fitness, and Walking for Fitness.

Harmful Substances

You can't look or feel your best if you are putting things in your body that are harmful. Taking drugs, like cocaine or marijuana, or sniffing glue, smoking cigarettes, and drinking alcohol affect your body in very negative ways.

Why You Should Say "No" to Harmful Substances

You might find that friends use harmful drugs and encourage you to join them. No matter what the reason for using drugs—to look more grown-up, to feel better, to be a part of the group, or to stop feeling bored—it's a mistake. You should say No! to harmful drugs, cigarettes, and alcohol because:

• You can become addicted. That means you need to take more and more or you can't stop when you want.

• Taking these substances can damage your body. For example, the chemicals in cigarettes can cause your blood flow to slow down and your heart to work harder. That's not good for your heart. And you can even get emphysema (a deadly disease that affects the lungs) or lung cancer. Women who smoke take another risk. If they smoke while pregnant, they can hurt their unborn baby.

• Taking these substances can affect the way you look, smell, and act. For example, smoking makes your hair, breath, and clothing smell and can cause you to get wrinkles around your mouth and on your face.

Find out more reasons why taking drugs, smoking cigarettes, and drinking alcohol are not wise. Then with your troop or group create a poster, quiz, or booklet to share with others.

More About Alcohol

A lot of kids take their first drink because friends pressure them. The alcohol in beer, wine, wine coolers, and liquor is very powerful. You can overdose and die from drinking too much alcohol! Some people who think they know exactly when to stop drinking fool themselves because alcohol is very sneaky. The part of the brain that would say "that's enough" or "time to stop" gets turned off by the alcohol. So you can easily drink too much and do some very foolish things.

Perhaps you've seen adults or even your parents drink alcohol from time to time. It's important to remember that many adults make responsible choices for themselves — which might include drinking in moderation — that children are not ready to make. It's never okay for a child or adolescent to make a decision for herself about drinking. For information about problems related to drinking, see page 59.

 It is very hard not to drink or smoke if your friends do. Read the section about "Peer Pressure" on pages 64–65. Practice some different ways you can let people know you don't want to drink or smoke cigarettes. If you want to know what to do about a family member's drug or alcohol problem, see page 59.

 Think of activities that you can do alone or with friends rather than just "hang out." Sometimes, you have to take a healthy risk and be the leader of your group by taking up a sport, hobby, or some other activity that would be a lot healthier than taking drugs. Look at Chapter Seven for ideas for different activities. Find three that look interesting, try them, and introduce them to your friends.

Stress

Stress is the way your body or mind reacts to people or situations that put demands on you physically, mentally, or emotionally. A fire alarm going off suddenly, an argument with your best friend, a piano recital—these are things that can cause stress. However, positive stress can help you do what you need to do every day, like work, play, and exercise. For example, positive stress is the feeling you may get before a test when you know you have studied. You feel a bit nervous but you are also more alert and ready for the test.

Everyone reacts in her own way to stress. Make note of what you do or how you feel when something stressful occurs. Do you have physical reactions: faster heartbeat, heavier and faster breathing, sweating, trembling, a dry mouth, weird feelings in your stomach, blushing or turning pale, a feeling of tightness or tension in your muscles? You and your troop can think about things that have been stressful to each of you and compare notes.

Managing Stress

When Stress Is Manageable

✔ You feel good, sometimes even great!
✔ Life can be hard sometimes, but you can handle it.
✔ You have more energy.
✔ You believe in yourself.
✔ You can learn new things.

When Stress Becomes Unmanageable

✔ You start to feel sick.
✔ Your stomach hurts.
✔ You get headaches.
✔ You feel tired.
✔ You don't feel like doing anything.
✔ You feel miserable.
✔ You feel like you can't take anymore!

Helpful Ways to Cope with Stress

✔ Face up to what's causing the stress.
✔ Express your feelings.
✔ Talk it over with someone you trust.
✔ Think about good things.
✔ Work with others to solve problems.
✔ Take a break!
✔ See if there's a way to reorganize things.
✔ See if there's another way to look at things that will help you accept them.
✔ Know that you can learn and grow from your mistakes.
✔ Treat your mind and body right: relax, exercise, sleep, eat well.

Responses That Don't Reduce Stress

✔ Ignore your feelings.
✔ Try to deal with it all by yourself.
✔ Just wish that it will go away by itself.
✔ Blame yourself.
✔ Think about only the bad things.
✔ Think that you're supposed to be perfect.
✔ Think that everything is wrong and needs to change.
✔ Treat your body badly with cigarettes, alcohol, drugs, undereating, or overeating.

Here is a relaxation activity you can try with your Girl Scout friends.

Sit comfortably in a chair, on the sofa, or on the floor. Close your eyes.

Imagine a place or thing that makes you feel calm. It could be a sunset, a poem that you especially like, a beautiful painting, a piece of music, the sound of the ocean.

Listen to and feel the sounds around you.

Listen to and feel your breathing. Keep it slow and steady. Breathe in through your nose and out through your mouth.

Each time you breathe out, imagine all the stress and tension leaving your body.

After ten minutes or so, slowly get up. Keep your breathing slow and steady.

Keep a journal to record events that cause stress. Note the ways you respond. Are they positive? Can you handle stress in more positive ways? Practice helpful ways to manage stress and find out what works for you.

In your troop or group discuss the stressful things that can happen to kids and teens. Discuss how to deal with stressful situations.

Exercise

One of the ways to care for your body is to exercise. Being fit helps improve physical and mental health and physical appearance. Make regular exercise a part of your life now—it's a good habit to keep as you get older.

Aerobic Exercise

Dancing, skating, jumping rope, bicycling, walking, running, and swimming are all aerobic activities because they have continuous movements that keep the heart beating faster. Your heart is a muscle.

By making the heart beat faster, you make it stronger. As your heart grows stronger, it takes less effort to do the same amount of physical work.

Discover how aerobic exercise helps your heart by doing some easy calculations. The illustration at the right shows how to measure your pulse rate. Take your pulse by placing your index and middle fingers on the inside of your wrist or on the carotid artery in your neck. Count the number of beats you feel for ten seconds. Multiply by six to get your pulse rate for one minute. Record that figure below.

Number of beats you feel for 10 seconds = ____ x 6 = ____ (pulse rate for one minute)

Now suppose through regular aerobic exercise you lower your pulse rate by two beats per minute. How many beats have you saved for an hour? a week? a year? Do you do at least one aerobic activity three times a week? If you do, you are getting the exercise your body needs to stay in shape and keep your heart healthy. *Note*: Before you start a regular exercise program you should get a physical check-up.

"To make yourself strong and healthy, it is necessary to begin with your inside, and to get the blood into good order and the heart to work well."
Juliette Gordon Low

Do an aerobic activity at least three times a week, for at least 20 or 30 minutes, with a friend. Plan on doing different types of activities, so you won't be bored. Walking is a very good exercise. You can play a favorite sport, too, as long as you are moving for at least 20 minutes. Some sports are more aerobic than others. Find out which are the most aerobic.

 With the help of a trained adult, organize an exercise class for other girls your age. Demonstrate and teach activities that can be used to warm up, work out, and cool down.

 An exercise journal is a good place to record your progress. Here is a sample:

Exercise Journal

Date: _____

Time: _____

Type of Exercise: _____

Your Partner: _____

Comments: _____

_____

Date: _____

Time: _____

Type of Exercise: _____

Your Partner: _____

Comments: _____

Nutrition

An important skill is choosing healthy foods. What you eat and drink affects your physical and mental health. Eating good foods and drinking enough water help your body grow, repair itself, and feel alert. How do you know what's nutritious?

The food pyramid, published by the United States Department of Agriculture, shows which proportion of foods to eat daily.

What do you learn about food groups by looking at the pyramid? Which foods should you eat the most? Less often? Think about the foods you eat. How would they fit in the food pyramid?

A Guide to Daily Food Choices

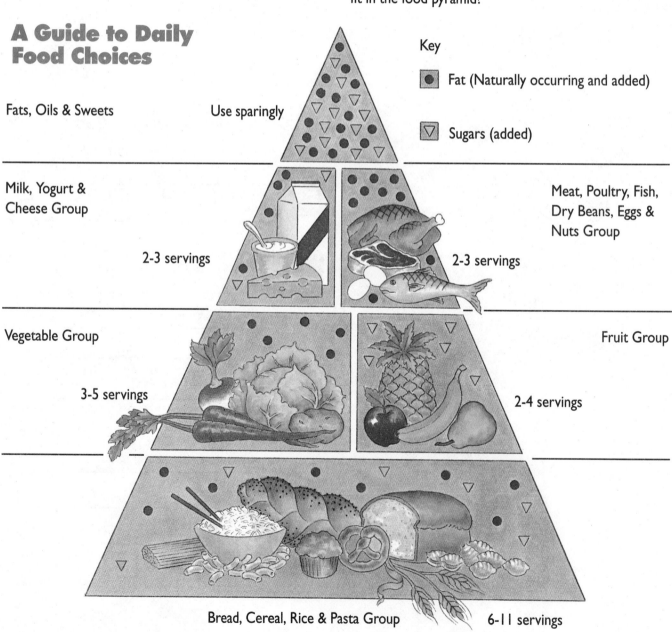

Key

● Fat (Naturally occurring and added)

▽ Sugars (added)

Fats, Oils & Sweets — Use sparingly

Milk, Yogurt & Cheese Group — 2-3 servings

Meat, Poultry, Fish, Dry Beans, Eggs & Nuts Group — 2-3 servings

Vegetable Group — 3-5 servings

Fruit Group — 2-4 servings

Bread, Cereal, Rice & Pasta Group — 6-11 servings

Prepare a healthy meal using the food-pyramid categories as a guide. Serve an appetizer, salad, main dish, and dessert.

Eat healthily by choosing snacks or lunches that are good for you. In your Girl Scout group or troop, sit in a circle. Each girl should write a snack or food that is not so healthy on a small slip of paper and put it into a bag or box. Take turns drawing a slip and brainstorming healthy substitutes. For example, if the snack was potato chips, you might suggest air-popped popcorn, rice cakes, or pita chips.

To make pita chips, separate pita-bread rounds into their two halves. Cut into sixths or eighths. Spray a cookie sheet with cooking oil and bake the pita slices at 350 degrees for 20 to 30 minutes—until crispy. You can sprinkle them with garlic powder, cinnamon-sugar, chili powder, or other flavorings. Use them as "dippers" for healthy, low-fat dips.

Food Labels

Foods that are processed—changed in some way or packaged or canned—may have chemicals added to make the foods taste fresher or to stay fresher longer. Many food products today are also artificially flavored to taste sweeter and artificially colored to look more attractive. Each American consumes about five pounds of chemical additives a year!

What can you do? You can learn how to read food labels and compare products. Labels provide a lot of information. Ingredients are listed in order from most to least. For example, if sugar is listed first, then that product contains more sugar than anything else.

Rules to Eat By

Follow these simple guidelines for nutritious eating. How could you share this information in an interesting way with younger girls or friends?

❶ Eat a balanced diet with plenty of dark green, yellow, and orange-colored fruits, vegetables, and grains.

❷ Eat food with fiber. Fiber comes from the cell walls in plants. Apples, beans, peas, oats, and barley are some foods that contain fiber.

❸ Reduce sugar, fat, and cholesterol. Sugar doesn't do much to help your body. In fact, it can decay teeth, it might hurt your heart, and it can make you gain weight. Did you know that sugar is found in foods under the names fructose, sucrose, dextrose, molasses, corn syrup, or honey?

❹ Maintain a healthy weight. If you eat right and get regular exercise, you can maintain a weight that is healthy for you.

❺ Reduce salt. Many Americans eat too many salty foods. Instead of eating salt, try experimenting with herbs and spices. Check food labels for sodium or salt.

❻ Drink lots of water—at least eight glasses of liquid a day, more if exercising. Remember soft drinks and some juices contain sugar and salt and may not be the best choices.

Collect labels from cans and boxes of a variety of products. Bring them to your Girl Scout meeting. Copy down the following information from each label:

total calories _____   protein _____

calories from fat _____   Vitamin A _____

sodium _____   Vitamin C _____

dietary fiber _____   calcium _____

sugars _____   iron _____

Compare labels and suggested serving sizes and look for the products that have the healthiest ingredients. Which foods are highest in fiber? Which foods have certain vitamins and minerals such as calcium and potassium? Which foods are lowest in sodium and fat? How can this information help you?

 Plan a group health feast. Each person can prepare and bring one type of healthy food to share. Then, enjoy!

 Create a troop or group recipe for a delicious, nutritious snack food. Prepare your snack for your meetings, for trips, or create colorful wrappers or packages and sell your snack as a troop money-earning project.

Careers in Health

Health-related careers are some of the fastest growing areas of employment. Not only is the need for people growing, but the types of jobs keep expanding as medical technology becomes more sophisticated.

 Here is a list of some health careers. How can you find out what people who have these jobs do? You could also discover what education or training is required and what the average salaries are.

Dental hygienist	Food and drug inspector
Physician	Hospital administrator
Recreation therapist	Midwife
Acupuncturist	Biomedical engineer
Chiropractor	Nutritionist
Nurse	Optician
Orthopedic surgeon	Oncologist
Periodontist	Physical therapist
Psychologist	Veterinarian

Being able to take care of yourself—whether it's by practicing a first-aid skill, preparing a healthy lunch, or organizing an exercise group—can make you feel good about yourself. And sometimes, there's no better feeling than simply feeling proud!

SKILLS TO USE EVERY DAY
CHAPTER 4

Taking Care of Your Clothes and Home

page 98

What's It Going to Be Like Working in the Future?

page 110

Money: Should You Spend It or Save It?

page 105

Running Late? Try Time Management

page 117

As you become older, you make more decisions for yourself and have more independence in your daily life. In this chapter, you'll learn about important life skills such as taking care of your clothes and home, managing money, and setting personal goals. Can you think of why these skills might be good to learn? Read on to discover the everyday skills you'd like to explore!

Taking Care of Your Clothes

Besides learning skills to care for and protect your body, you also need to learn how to care for the place where you live, the things you own, and the clothes you wear. Learning how to repair your clothing, how to handle tools, and how to do simple repairs helps build your self-confidence. It feels good to know that you can do these things for yourself.

Clothing-Buying Checklist

★ Is the clothing machine- or hand-washable or "dry clean only"? (Dry cleaning costs more than washing.)

★ Does the fabric wrinkle easily? (Squeeze it to find out.)

★ Is the clothing something you can wear often?

★ Does it go with other clothes you have?

★ Are there extra buttons?

★ If it needs to be altered, is it a simple alteration you can do yourself like sew a hem? (See pages 101–102 for sewing instructions.)

Clothes That Fit and Look Good

Whether buying or making clothes, it is important to know what looks good and what fits correctly. As you grow older, your measurements will vary. Remember there is no such thing as a perfect size. You might wear a Children's (6–14), Pre-teen's, Junior, Junior Petite, Misses, or Women's size.

No matter how much you spend on your clothing, consider whether the clothing is worth the cost. You can spend a little money or a lot of money, but you do want clothing that is well made. To help you make decisions while shopping, look at the clothing-buying checklist above.

and Your Home ▲▲▲▲▲▲▲▲▲▲▲

Washing and Drying Your Clothes

Whether you're washing your clothes by machine or hand, keep these instructions in mind:

★ Be sure to read clothing labels for care and cleaning instructions. Some will say "dry clean only," while others will say "hand-washable" or "machine-washable."

★ Follow the instructions on the inside label of the clothing to select water temperature, as well as the type of washing. (Some instructions may say "delicate cycle," "permanent press," or "regular wash." These apply to different types of machine washing.)

★ Close all zippers before washing.

★ Empty the contents of pockets before washing.

★ Check for stains and rub a small amount of laundry detergent or pre-washing liquid on those spots. It may be necessary to soak clothing if it has a heavy stain.

★ Follow the directions on the detergent box to determine how much detergent to use.

★ Follow directions on the washing machine to determine when and how to add the laundry detergent. (In some machines, you add detergent directly to the water; in others, you add detergent to a basket or opening.)

★ Some clothing can be washed in a machine but not dried in a clothes dryer. Read the label to see if you should lay the clothing flat to dry.

Clothing Care Symbols	
Symbol	**Meaning**
⌄	Wash
△	Bleach
□	Tumble Dry
(iron)	Iron
(iron crossed out)	Do not iron
○	Dryclean
⊗	Do not dryclean

HANDBOOK ACTIVITY Think of a way you can organize and care for your clothing so that your clothing stays neat and is easy to find in the morning. If you do not wash your own clothes, with an adult's permission, try machine washing or hand washing your clothing for a week.

Fashion designers can become very famous, but there are lots of other jobs in the fashion industry. Find out about careers in the fashion and cosmetic industries. Some suggestions are: clothing buyer, fashion consultant, personal shopper, cosmetologist, hairstylist, textile designer, salesperson. How can you find out about these careers? Maybe you can interview people who have these jobs or career shadow them for a day.

 Put on a fashion show with a theme. You might want to dress for different themes: Fashions for the Outdoors, Fashions for the Future, Fashions for Different Careers, Fashions for Parties. What other themes can you create?

Quick and Easy

Keep your clothes looking new and neat by sewing simple repairs. First you need sewing supplies.

 Choose a container (metal, like a cookie tin, or sturdy cardboard, like a shoe box) to make a sewing kit. Design and decorate with paper, paints, or fabric. These are some items you should have in your sewing kit:

★ **A package of sharp, assorted needles (the bigger the size number of the needle the smaller the eye of the needle, and the finer the point)**

★ **A thimble—to protect your finger**

★ **A small box of straight pins**

★ **A pair of scissors or shears**

★ **Spools of thread—of different colors and thicknesses (heavy-duty thread is great for sewing on buttons)**

★ **A pin cushion**

★ **A small ruler or measuring tape**

★ **Iron-on patches**

Mend-Its ▲ ▲ ▲ ▲ ▲ ▲ ▲ ▲ ▲ ▲ ▲ ▲ ▲ ▲

Sewing Stitches

Before stitching, thread your needle by carefully pushing the thread through the eye of the needle. Once it goes through, pull about four inches of thread through. Knot the longer end of the thread.

The diagrams on this page show the basic sewing stitches. Before sewing, pin your fabric in place with straight pins. Remember, the thimble makes it easy to push the needle through the fabric and protects the finger doing the pushing.

★ Hemming stitch—for hemming pants, dresses, skirts, tops. (See next page.)

★ Basting stitch—for holding the fabric in place before doing the final sewing by hand or machine.

★ Running stitch—for sewing straight seams.

★ Blanket stitch—to make a decorative edge that also prevents unraveling.

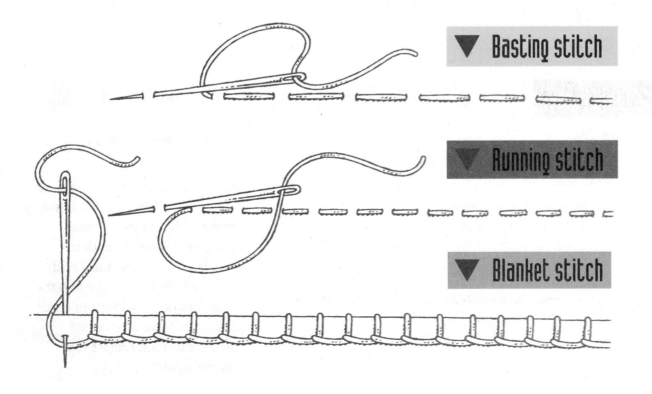

▼ Basting stitch

▼ Running stitch

▼ Blanket stitch

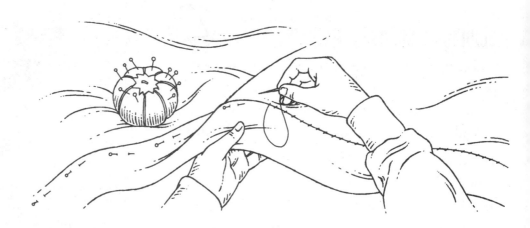

Make a Hem

Fold up the bottom of the skirt 1/4 inch (1/2 cm). Then fold the hem up to the length you want, usually one or two inches. A heavy fabric can take a bigger hem and a light fabric should have a smaller hem. Pin the hem and try the garment on to make sure the hem is even. Check the back and front in a mirror. Sew with the hemming stitch on the inside. Keep your stitches as tiny as possible so they don't show on the outside.

 Mend a piece of your own clothing or ask permission to mend a member of your family's clothing.

 Learn more about embroidery on page 157. Create a troop project that uses your sewing skills.

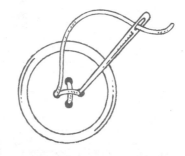

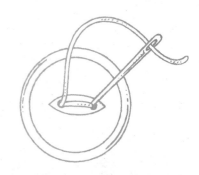

▲ Two-Holed Button

▲ Four-Holed Button

▲ Button on a Coat

Replace a Button

Mark the place for a button with two straight pins unless the original holes made by the thread are easy to see.

Start from underneath and pull your thread through the fabric and then through a hole in the button, then down through another hole and through the fabric.

Repeat this six to eight times—more if it is a coat or jacket—and tie off the thread on the wrong side.

The illustrations show the stitches for a two-holed button, a four-holed button, and a button on a coat.

Repair a Rip or Add a Fashion Patch

Cut a piece of fabric to a size about 1/2 inch (1 1/4 cm) wider than the rip or hole. Use the blanket stitch around the edges to attach to clothing. You can also use a ready-made iron-on patch. Just follow the directions on the package to attach this patch. Novelty stores sell different patches. Express your fashion style!

Simple Home Repairs ▲▲▲▲▲▲▲

 CAUTION!

Caring for your home by making repairs is another important life skill. You can learn to make simple repairs with the right tools, an adult's help, and some practice. First become familiar with some tool-safety tips:

TIPS FOR TOOL SAFETY

safety tips

- Always make certain you have completely learned how to use a tool before you start working with it.
- Never use power tools unless an adult who knows how to use them is present.
- Make sure you have a clear and steady work surface.
- Keep tools out of reach of younger children.
- Make sure the tools you are using are in good condition.
- Wear goggles to protect your eyes, particularly if you are hammering, sawing, or drilling.

Hammer–for pounding and removing nails.
Make sure the hammer is the right weight for you. You should be able to hold it comfortably near the end of the handle. Raise the hammer with a backward flip of your wrist and then a forward flip.

Saw–for cutting wood or metal.
You will probably use a common saw, or cross cut, for most projects. Use one that is about 16 inches long or slightly longer, depending on your reach.

Plane–for making wood smooth or for making wood just a bit smaller.
Use a plane that fits comfortably in your hands. Be sure your board is in a vise (a tool that grips the wood) to make it steady. Use both hands and move the plane in one direction only.

Sandpaper–for smoothing rough surfaces.
Sandpaper can be wrapped around and thumbtacked to a block of wood to make it steady. Coarse sandpaper should be used for your first sanding; then gradually move to finer grains for finishing.

Screwdriver–for turning screws that hold things together.
In the illustration you can see two types of screwdrivers. Each type works with a particular kind of screw.

Awl–for making holes.
An awl is good to mark the place where you want to put a nail or for starting the hole where you will put a screw.

Pliers–for gripping things.
Pliers can help you make things tight or loosen things that are stuck.

Wrench–for turning nuts and bolts.
A wrench makes nuts and bolts tight or loose.

Level–for making things straight.

A level is used to keep angles and edges straight.

Standard

Phillips head

Drill–for making deep holes.
The illustrations show a power drill and a hand drill. While all tools can hurt you when not used properly, drills can be extra dangerous, so make sure you follow the tool-safety tips before using one.

Hand Drill

Power Drill

Maintaining Your Home

 Do you know how to:

- ✔ Wash a window?
- ✔ Change the linens on a bed?
- ✔ Replace a vacuum cleaner bag?
- ✔ Program a VCR?
- ✔ Use a microwave oven?
- ✔ Turn off the water in an emergency?
- ✔ Install a shower head?

- ✔ Repot a plant?
- ✔ Shampoo carpeting?
- ✔ Use an extension cord properly?
- ✔ Clean a bathtub, toilet, or tile floors?
- ✔ Check a car's tires for air?
- ✔ Check the level of oil in a car?
- ✔ Remove stains from upholstery or carpeting?

 Choose three things from the list at the left and, in your Girl Scout group or troop or with an adult, demonstrate that you know how to do them.

Tool Kit

 Put together a home tool kit and practice using your tools:

- ❧ Use a level and a hammer to hang a picture.
- ❧ Use sandpaper to fix a door or window that sticks.
- ❧ Use a screwdriver or wrench to tighten screws or bolts that have become loose.
- ❧ Use a wrench to replace a washer in a leaky faucet.

Doing Repairs

 Find someone to show you how to do these home repairs:

- ❧ Fix a hole in a window screen.
- ❧ Fix a loose chair or table leg.
- ❧ Install batteries in a flashlight or smoke detector.
- ❧ Caulk around a bathtub, shower, window, or door.
- ❧ Unclog a sink, bathtub, or toilet.
- ❧ Replace the cord on an electrical appliance.
- ❧ Repair a crack in a wall.
- ❧ Repair broken pottery.
- ❧ Repair a broken window shade or venetian blind.

Managing Money

Do you get an allowance? Do you earn money baby-sitting or delivering newspapers? Have you ever gotten money as a gift? How do you decide what to do with money–save it, spend it, or donate it to a worthy cause? As you grow older, you will make more decisions about money. One place to begin learning good money-management skills is in your Girl Scout troop or group.

Troop or Group Dues and Money-Earning Projects

As a Junior Girl Scout, you make decisions about how to earn and use the money in your Girl Scout troop or group. Money from dues or earned through special projects is money for you to spend on Girl Scout activities.

Girl Scout troops and groups need money for all kinds of things: project supplies, trips, games, books, equipment, donations. Girl Scout troops and groups often set up a troop treasury, depositing money from troop or group dues and money-earning projects.

Troop or Group Dues

The members of your troop or group agree on an amount of money that everyone can afford. A troop's or group's dues may be $.10, $.25, $1.00; there is no one best amount. The troop or group also must decide: How often will dues be collected? Who will collect them? Where will the money be kept? How will the dues be used?

Often, this is decided in the beginning of the year when the troop or group sets its budget. You can also agree to raise the dues if you are saving for a special project, or lower the dues if you have enough money in the treasury. Remember the section about troop or group government on pages 24–25? How have you set up your troop or group government? How is your troop or group money collected and recorded?

Keeping Track of Troop or Group Dues

Your troop or group should have an easy and clear way of keeping track of money and equipment. You could use a budget like the one here or set up your own system. Every time money is collected or spent, it must be recorded and new totals must be figured out. This recording should be the responsibility of the troop treasurer. Whenever money is collected, it should be counted, recorded, and then put in a safe place. The best place to keep your troop or group money is in a checking account in a bank.

Your troop or group should set up a budget as soon as you have decided on the amount of troop or group dues. Make sure to include money left in your troop or group treasury from last year. Keep a special book or ledger for your budget. Your treasurer or troop or group leader can be responsible for bringing the ledger to each meeting. Part of your troop's or group's business at meetings will be a report from the treasurer on the amount of money in the account.

Troop or Group Budget

INCOME		EXPENSES	
Dues	_____	Supplies	_____
Product Sales	_____	Transportation	_____
Money-Earning Projects	_____	Fees (for example, for admissions)	_____
Contributions (from parents, sponsors, etc.)	_____	Refreshments	_____
Money from Last Year	_____	Recognitions	_____
Others	_____	Others	_____

Whenever your troop or group buys something with this money, it should save all receipts and sales slips. Deduct what has been spent from the total.

Money-Earning Projects

Girl Scout troops and groups often organize and carry out an activity to earn money for the treasury. Many troops participate in the annual Girl Scout cookie or calendar sales.

HANDBOOK ACTIVITY

In your troop or group, practice your sales skills and your money manager skills. Think of different situations and what you could say. Figure out how much money you will earn and what you can do with it.

Baby-sitting
Gift-wrapping
Car or bike wash

Recycling drive

Craft or baked-goods sale
Pet-sitting or plant-sitting

Neighborhood landscaping:
weeding, lawn mowing,
planting, etc.

Selling Girl Scout Cookies

Junior Girl Scouts may decide to work on the Girl Scout cookie sale. As part of your troop or group, you want to contribute your talents and skills. Decide what you would like to learn about selling. There are many different jobs involved in a cookie sale. You can sell cookies. You can help organize cookie boxes and keep track of the money. Maybe you will be a part of a group that sells cookies at a shopping mall or in the lobby of an office building.

Decisions about what each person can do will be made in your troop or group.

If you decide to sell cookies, discuss and practice safety rules in your troop or group. Safety rules apply to any money-earning project. Be sure you follow the rules. You should also know some salesperson skills:

$ Learn about what you are selling so you can answer customers' questions.

$ Know what your Girl Scout troop or group is planning to do with the money it earns. What special things do Girl Scouts do?

$ Let the customer know how much money she owes you, when you will be collecting this money, and when she can expect to get the cookies and other products. Make sure you give customers the cookies and other products on the day promised.

$ Always say thank-you, even if someone doesn't buy anything. People will remember your good manners, which is important because you are representing Girl Scouts and yourself.

Other Money-Earning Projects

What are some other money-earning projects? Look at the column of ideas on this page. Do any ideas capture your interest? Add some of your own ideas.

Many of these activities can provide your troop or group with enough money to take a trip or carry out a service project. Before doing any money-earning activity though, you and your troop or group members must get permission from your parents or guardians. Your troop or group leader must get permission from the local Girl Scout council. Be sure also to find out about any safety rules, as well as local laws, or health department regulations, that could affect your activity.

Budgeting

Budgeting helps you decide where and how to spend money. Learning how to keep a budget is one of the most important money-management skills you can learn.

Look at the budget sheet below. Fixed expenses are those that hardly ever change.

Flexible expenses you can control. To use the budget sheet, fill in the amount of money you expect to have for each week (Week 1, Week 2, Week 3). Then record the amount you plan to spend in each category. At the end of the week, write in the amount you actually spent.

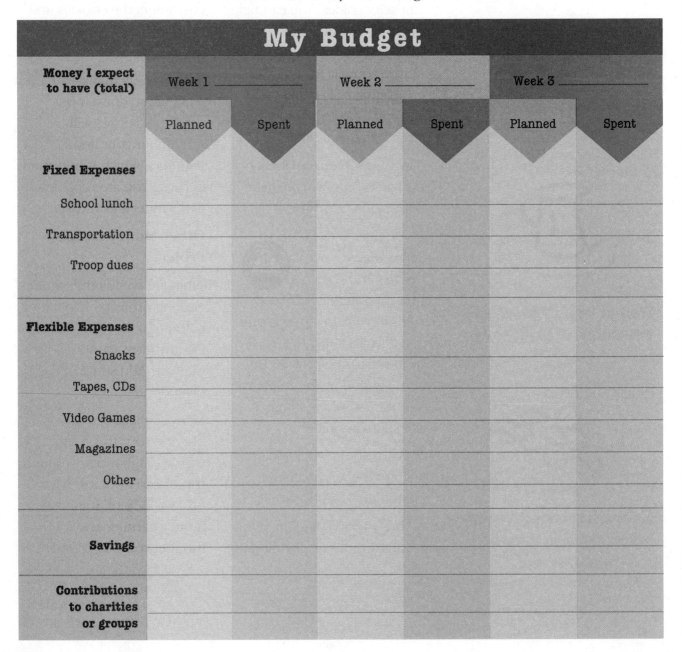

My Budget

Money I expect to have (total)	Week 1 _____		Week 2 _____		Week 3 _____	
	Planned	Spent	Planned	Spent	Planned	Spent
Fixed Expenses						
School lunch						
Transportation						
Troop dues						
Flexible Expenses						
Snacks						
Tapes, CDs						
Video Games						
Magazines						
Other						
Savings						
Contributions to charities or groups						

If you want to save money, decrease the amount you are spending on flexible expenses. How long can you stick to your budget? See if you can follow it for at least two months.

More About Money

Keeping money in a savings account is one way to keep your money safe. Once you have opened a savings account, the bank keeps a record of how much you deposit (put in), withdraw (take out), and the amount of interest earned (money the bank pays you for holding your money). Different banks give different amounts of interest.

Checking accounts are bank accounts from which you can sign a written order (a check) that tells the bank to pay a certain amount of money from your account to the person or company named on the check.

Here's your imaginary checking account. Imagine that for a month you have saved: two dollars out of your allowance ($2.00 per week), gift money ($20.00), and job money ($15.00). What is your total?

_____

 How much do you know about credit cards? Learn about the interest charged by credit-card companies and stores.

 Visit a bank and find out how to open a savings and a checking account. Find out what other services are offered.

 Help your family with a household budget. What expenses are flexible? What expenses are fixed?

 Invite someone who works in the financial industry, an accountant, a bank officer, a bank examiner, or a personal finance manager to visit your troop or group and explain what she does.

Now consider the amounts you would withdraw by writing checks. There's a special celebration coming up at school and the suggested donation is $4.00. You also want to pay your Girl Scout troop or group dues for the month (multiply your weekly troop dues by 4.3). What is your total? _____

Use your budget to help figure out the other expenses for which you would have to write checks. What is your balance (the amount left in your account)?

_____

When you make another deposit, add it to your balance. Whenever you write a check to make a withdrawal, subtract it from your balance.

Exploring Careers

What's it going to be like working in the future?

There are a zillion jobs that were not around when your grandparents, or even your parents, were growing up. If you were to fast-forward into your future, you might be amazed at the jobs people will be doing and at the places people will be working.

The workplaces of tomorrow will link people through vast computer and communication networks across the country and around the world. You may need to work at night because the people with whom you do business are in a different time zone.

If you'd like to further investigate the work of the future...

 Interview three different women who work in companies with more than 100 people. Find out about work benefits. What changes would they like to see in the future? Interview several women who are self-employed and ask the same questions.

Whenever you think of possible careers or jobs, think about your skills and abilities, your characteristics, your goals, your values, and your interests. All help shape the ideal career for you.

Skills and Abilities

You probably do some things better than other things. Are you athletic? Are you artistic? Are you good at helping people get along? The special skills and abilities you have can help you find a career.

 Choose five activities from Chapter Seven and brainstorm a list of careers that could match those activities.

Someone who is athletic may do well as a coach, a physical therapist, or an aerobics instructor. Someone who is artistic may enjoy being an interior designer, architect, or film editor. Remember, while you seem to be born with some abilities, as you grow you add new skills.

Right now you may feel uncomfortable speaking in front of a group. Does that rule out a career as a teacher, corporate trainer, or broadcaster? No! Maybe you will become a patrol leader, run for student government, or become active in an environmental cause. You discover that it's not so difficult to speak to a group about something you believe. You might give a speech about Girl Scouting at a school assembly during Girl Scout Week. Each time you give a speech, it gets a little easier. Soon, you are able to add public speaking to your list of skills and abilities.

Your Characteristics

Are you quiet or outgoing? emotional or calm? a quick or slow decision-maker? Do you prefer to work alone or with a group? Your characteristics affect your career choice. A person who prefers to work alone might choose a job as a computer software designer or a truck driver rather than a

_____

_____

_____

_____

_____

_____

_____

_____

Skills and Abilities I Wish I Had

_____

_____

_____

_____

_____

_____

_____

_____

(What can you do to help your wishes come true?)

police officer or a stockbroker. An air traffic controller needs to be a quick decision-maker. A counselor should be calm and reassuring. Just like your skills and abilities, your characteristics can change as you grow older.

My Characteristics

_____

_____

_____

_____

_____

_____

Think of women you admire. What characteristics do they have that you would like to have?

Characteristics I Would Like to Have

_____

_____

_____

_____

_____

_____

Values

Read about values on pages 48–52. List those values that might influence your choice of career. Write them here.

_____

_____

_____

_____

For example, if one of your values is to be close to your family, you may not want a job that involves a lot of traveling. If you value independence or adventure, you may look for a job as a salesperson or consultant in which you'd travel a lot.

Your Interests

Lots of times your interests flow from your skills and abilities, your values, and your characteristics. A person who enjoys playing soccer may be athletic. A person who belongs to a choir may be a good singer. A person who goes white-water rafting may value adventure. Your interests may also reflect things you would like to do better. You might not be the greatest athlete, but you love to do things in a group and you love being outdoors, so you joined the after-school soccer league. Your interests should be things you enjoy doing.

Sometimes, you might feel pressured to go along with your friends' interests, even though you'd prefer to do something else. Read "Jamela the Future Scientist." Has this ever happened to you?

What would you tell Jamela? How can you finish her story? Why do other people make it hard for you to do what you want? What are some of the different things Jamela can do or say? Act them out; then, in your troop or group, vote on the best responses.

You might hear that girls can't have certain interests–like doing carpentry or playing football. Or you may be told that the most popular kids aren't on the swimming team, they're on the basketball team. It is hard, sometimes, to follow your own interests without pressure from others. But, you are a

unique and special person. And while you may share some interests with friends, you should feel good about doing things without friends' approval.

You might still hear people saying that some jobs are only for men and other jobs only for women. Some people are very old-fashioned! Women are doing lots of jobs today and will continue to be an important part of the workforce. Some jobs, such as secretary, teacher, or bank teller have traditionally been women's jobs. It is great if you want to be a bank teller. But, if you want to be a certified public accountant or bank examiner, you should not become a bank teller because

Jamela the Future Scientist

you believe only men can be bankers or accountants.

It is wrong to be discouraged from taking math courses because of the myth that girls don't do well in math. That's simply not true! Girls are great at math, science, and computers! It is important to believe this because jobs that require strong backgrounds in math, science, or computers almost always pay more than jobs that don't require that knowledge. Here is a list of some jobs that require college math or science courses.

Why not look in the classified advertisements of a newspaper or phone the professional associations or some businesses and find out how much a person makes who has one of these jobs? Compare these salaries with some of the more traditional "female" jobs. Is this fair?

- ✍ Accountant
- ✍ Economist
- ✍ Psychologist
- ✍ Statistician
- ✍ Computer Software Designer
- ✍ Architect
- ✍ Stock Broker
- ✍ Recycling Coordinator
- ✍ Physician
- ✍ Pilot
- ✍ Buyer
- ✍ Actuary
- ✍ Park Ranger
- ✍ Engineer

Dorthea Brown:*

Expert Systems Specialist

Dorthea Brown is one woman combining a career in technology with the responsibilities of a family. She works as a specialist in expert systems–a kind of computer programming that copies how an expert makes decisions and solves problems.

As an expert systems specialist, Dorthea looks for tools to help people do their work better. A computer is programmed to copy the decision-making process of an expert. That helps people in a company do their job better because they can tap into the knowledge of experts who may not always be available.

Dorthea recommends that all students get a broad exposure to the sciences. She encourages taking courses in chemistry, biology, physics, and basic math even though their usefulness may not be clear at first. Dorthea offers these suggestions: "Take risks in subjects–don't just stick with what you already do well. Challenge yourself, and study things you can learn from."

After the birth of her son, T.J., Dorthea and her husband, Thomas, had to make some tough decisions about careers and family responsibilities. Some people choose day care or family providers, but the Browns felt that one of them should be home during the day with their son. So, for the time being, Thomas has put his career on hold and stays home with T.J., while Dorthea pursues her career. The Browns are fortunate that they can afford to live on one salary. Dorthea feels that her husband's support has been critical to her success. If Dorthea and Thomas decide to change roles, they will work together to do what is best for their family.

In the future, more women will be involved in the fields of science and technology, a growing job market because so much is changing. To be part of this change, seek out classes in science, computers, and math. Look for experiences that give you a taste of what science and technology are all about, like earning Girl Scout badges in the World of Today and Tomorrow, visiting science museums, and volunteering in places that can give you practical experience.

Interview someone in the field of science and technology, such as a computer salesperson, a researcher, a futurist (someone who studies the future and makes predictions based upon current trends), a science reporter, or a telephone company employee. Find out what changes they are predicting for the next five years, ten years, twenty years.

Find out about a career you might like to have. Find out about education, special training, and salary (beginning and after ten years). What clothes, tools, or equipment are used in this career? To what other careers does this career lead? If you and the other girls in your troop or group find out about different careers, think of ways to share or use this information

* Dorthea Brown is not a real person, but her story describes one kind of a choice a woman might make.

Your Goals

What are some of your goals? You might have a short-term goal–I want to finish my homework before 8 p.m. You might have a long-term goal– I want to practice my violin so I can enter a special music high school. You need to think about your lifetime goals when you are thinking about a career. How can you combine a career and family life? Is it important to earn a lot of money? Some jobs pay more than others. Think about the kind of life you would like to have. Would you rather live in a city or in the country? Forestry might be a good field for someone who loves the country, and oceanography might be perfect for someone who loves the sea. Your goals may change as you get older and you may switch careers more than once during your lifetime.

Use this chart to help plan personal or troop or group goals.

Goal: _____

Steps to Reach This Goal:

1._____

2._____

3._____

Planned Date of Completion for Each Step:

1._____

2._____

3._____

People Who Can Help Me: _____

_____

I Will Reach This Goal by: _____
(date)

If you did not reach your goal by the date set, think about the following:

·Was my goal too hard for me to reach now? Do I need to spend more time on it?

·Do I need the help of others to reach this goal?

·Should I choose different steps that will help me?

·Am I still interested in this goal–or have my goals changed?

_____

_____

_____

_____

_____

Your Future

Here's some space to record your thoughts and dreams for the future. You might want to save this page and look back at it when you are older.

115

Doing Your Best in School

Staying in school is one of the most important things you can do to reach your goals, but school does much more than prepare you for a career. School is a place where you learn to get along with different people. It gives you opportunities to win and lose, be a leader and a follower, try new experiences, and discover what you like and dislike.

School prepares you to be an adult. Skills such as writing a report or studying for a test will help you as a grown-up as you will need to read, write, and study information in your job or career. Your math and reading skills will help you find out which car gets the best gas mileage or which air conditioner uses the least electricity.

 Work and Study Habits

Some people get good marks very easily; others may have to work hard to get good grades. And wherever you fall in that range, you can feel good about schoolwork when you know you are doing your personal best. Here are some pointers to help you do your best.

At School

If you find your schoolwork getting a bit rough, you can:

✔ Ask the teacher for extra help.
✔ Ask for a tutor.
✔ Set up a study group with your classmates or other friends. Compare and review each other's notes. A Girl Scout troop can be wonderful help in this way!

Don't be afraid to ask questions, especially when you don't understand something! Don't worry about what others might think–chances are they don't understand it either. The only silly question is the one that never gets asked!

Don't be afraid to make a mistake. School is a great place to learn from your mistakes.

At Home

Use a large wall or desk calendar to help track assignments, especially reports and tests. This will help you pace yourself and remind you to do some work each day. Use stickers to mark special days or days when assignments are due.

Perhaps one of the most important things you can do is develop a winning attitude. You may not be on the very top, but you should try to do your personal best. Knowing you've tried can really boost your self-esteem.

Managing Time

You will always have to make decisions about how to spend your time. Time management, like stress management and money management, is a skill you can learn. To manage time wisely you need to think about priorities (the things that are most important to you).

Make a list of all the things you did this week. What did you do at school? at home? Did you play sports? Spend time with friends? Make your list as complete as possible.

Now, examine your list and:

✔ Put an X next to all those things you had no choice about doing. For example, you had to sleep and get dressed.

✔ Put an H next to those things that made you feel happy or calm.

✔ Put an F next to those things that made you feel close to your family.

✔ Put a B next to those things that exercised your body.

Look over the list now. Circle those things you could spend less time doing.

What pattern can you see from your list? What kinds of activities are you doing the most? Are your activities balanced? What would you want to do more often? less often? Compare your list with other girls in your Girl Scout troop or group. How could a list like this (with different categories) be useful for planning Girl Scout meeting activities?

Make a list of what you need to get done. Your list could be for an evening, a day, or a week. Once you have the list written, put a * next to those things that are most important. Do those things first. As you finish each thing on your list, cross it off. You'll feel good when you see how much you have accomplished.

Procrastination

Procrastination—putting off doing what you have to do—is a bad habit many people share. For example, on Monday you learn that you have a social studies test on Thursday. That means you have to study your notes and read four chapters in your textbook. But, Thursday seems a long time away, so on Monday evening you chat on the phone with your girlfriend for an hour and watch television until 10:00 p.m. On Tuesday, your mom asks you to watch your younger brother after school. You feel you need a reward after doing that for three hours (he wasn't still for a second!), so once your mom gets home you go to your girlfriend's house to listen to music and practice some dance moves. Now it's Wednesday and the test is tomorrow. No more procrastinating! The problem is now you feel stressed because you have so much studying to do. What would have been a better way to prepare for the test?

There are lots of ways to manage time:

• You could have broken the work into sections and studied a little bit each day.

• You could have divided the work in half and studied Tuesday and Wednesday.

• You could have studied your notes while on the bus or standing on line somewhere.

Being Media Wise

Look back at your time management list. How much time was spent watching television? playing video games? watching movies? watching music videos? reading magazines or newspapers? Television, newspapers, and magazines are called media–sources of news and information.

Media Influences

No matter how much or how little you watch television or read magazines, you are influenced by media. Think of what you know about a major city. Besides the information in textbooks, your knowledge and opinions will be affected by what you see on the nightly news and by what you hear on the radio or read in a newspaper. Maybe you hear mostly about crime in that city or maybe you read about its money troubles. You might discover, though, that if you visit that city, it is very different from the way it has been shown in the media.

So much happens in any one day and the media can only report on a small amount of all that happens. What appears on the nightly news or on the front page of the newspaper is chosen by an editor or a group of editors or producers. By choosing one story or another, these people are influencing what you will know–and won't know. Also, the different types of media are competitive. Everyone wants to be first with an exciting story. After it appears, other media will repeat the same story, perhaps adding information.

Besides wanting to give you information, the owners of newspapers and magazines want to sell more newspapers and magazines and the owners of television stations want you to watch their news programs. So you might see or read stories that are run more to get your attention than to give you information. Which story do you think a newspaper would put on its front page? A story about a T.V. star being hospitalized or a story that reprints a senator's speech to a local business group? The senator's speech could contain very important information on the local economy, new taxes, or new jobs which the community needs to know, but often, the story about the T.V. star, a less important story, would be placed first.

 If you can get a copy of two or more newspapers printed on the same day, choose one story printed in both and compare. Where does the story appear? the front page? page 12? in a different section? How long is the story? Is the information the same? What is the tone–the overall impression–of the story? positive, negative, neutral, anxious, upbeat?

 Watch two news shows shown on television at the same time. Flip back and forth between the shows. Keep a log of what stories are reported, how much time is given to the story, who reports the story (the main newscaster or a reporter), and what differs in the report. Compare your log with other girls in your Girl Scout troop or group.

Television

In some families, the television is on most of the day. Other families may not own a television. If you watch television (and chances are you do since the average viewing time for an American family is about seven hours a day), you and your family have the power to choose what shows you will watch. Television shows can excite your imagination, give you new solutions to problems, teach you a new skill, or can bore you, have unbelievable characters, or contain a lot of violence. How do you decide which shows to watch?

 With your family or in your troop or group, create guidelines for television viewing. You could also develop similar guidelines for video games. Here are some points to consider:

- How much television can be watched on school nights and how much on the weekends?

- Do real people behave the way characters on the show behave? How does the behavior differ?

- Does the show contain violence? If it does, how does it fit into the story? Is it unnecessary?

- Does the show contain sexual situations? Does your family have rules about your watching these shows?

- Add your own ideas to the list.

Try creating a Smart Music-Video Viewing Guide for you and your friends. Create your own awards or seal of approval for videos that meet your standards. What standards can you set? (A standard is a rule or model.) One standard could be not to allow violence. Other standards could be to limit bad language or to allow only positive portrayals of women and girls.

Advertisements

The media is also the means by which advertisers tell you about their products. Think about what makes you buy products, like clothes or CDs or tapes. You probably make buying decisions based on advertisements. Even if you feel you do not pay much attention to commercials or ads, they do surround you with jingles (songs in a commercial) and phrases that stick in your head: "Buy 'Hair So Beautiful' Shampoo–the One for a New and Exciting You."

 Close your eyes for a moment. What advertisement pops into your head? Why do you remember it? How does this advertisement try to persuade you? In your troop or group, gather in small groups or pairs and pick an advertisement or commercial to analyze (study carefully). Think of three ways the advertisement is persuasive. Are there attractive people in the advertisement? Does the advertisement promise something new? What are some other messages the advertisement is sending? Pick one person in your group or pair to explain to the others what you discovered.

Advertisers try to convince you that a product is safe for the environment, good for your health, or fun to use, eat, or drink. They would like you to believe that you will be more popular, attractive, successful, happy, or rich if you buy the product. Unfortunately, it is a very unusual product that can do all those things! While advertising can be helpful when you are making buying decisions, you also have to think carefully about what the product can really do.

Learning everyday skills such as doing repairs, setting career goals, and managing money can be a challenge. Which everyday skills did you enjoy learning most? Why not pick out five or six skills you've learned and include them in a "Skills Log."

Skills I've Learned	How I Did It
1. How to open a bank account	Read the section on managing money. Went to the bank with my Girl Scout leader. Talked to a bank officer. She helped me deposit money.
2. How to repot a plant	Watched and helped Uncle Charlie do gardening. Decided to work on "Plants and Animals" badge. Shared with my troop my observations about how plants grow; also showed everyone how to repot a plant.

Use this sample to create your own Skills Log. Why do you think it's important to learn new skills?

120

EVERYONE IS DIFFERENT

Imagine if everyone looked the same, ate the same food, and had the same interests. Life would be pretty boring, wouldn't it? This chapter will be about differences in people—celebrating all groups and dealing with problems that come up when people don't respect each other. Do you have any ideas for helping people get along? If you do, start writing them down to use in some of the activities ahead.

121

National Forum on Kids and Prejudice

Imagine being chosen to attend a meeting of kids from across the United States interested in helping people get along better. Let's meet the participants at an imaginary National Forum on Kids and Prejudice. Find out how they tried to make a difference.

The whole group is meeting for the first time. Yvonne and Bernadette had been chosen as coordinators and had met the day before to do some planning. Everyone in the group was interested in helping people get along better, but no one was sure where to start.

YVONNE: Since I picked the card that said Facilitator, I guess I'll start facilitating...

SHAWN: Let's set some rules, first.

YVONNE: Like no interrupting! But, that's a good idea. We already thought about how to do this. Bernadette, you brought your notes with you?

BERNADETTE: I have them right here. Welcome everybody to our first National Forum on Kids and Prejudice. Some of you may feel uncomfortable talking about this subject, so we thought we should all discuss setting some ground rules—and everyone has to agree to them. No exceptions, right?

ROBERTO: She's tough!

ANDREA: What are you saying—girls can't be tough??? Maybe we have our first stereotype. And we haven't even been here a minute!!

ROBERTO: I was joking, okay?

LIN: That's part of the problem: jokes that make fun of people because of their race or because of anything— age, gender, abilities.

BERNADETTE: We're not saying you can't have a sense of humor; lots of times that helps a tense situation. But, ethnic jokes are wrong. Any joke that puts people down is not funny. Anyway, let's go over our rules. We're here to make a plan to fight prejudice—starting with ourselves and then working in our communities. We're hoping to leave with some practical steps we can all take. But, because we're starting with us—what's inside—we thought it was important that what we say in this room stays in this room. No going back and telling your crowd at school what so and so said at the forum. Everyone agree?

MAILE: That's really important. We have to trust each other enough to be able to share our feelings—and that's hard enough to do without thinking someone's going to be telling the whole world afterwards.

BERNADETTE: Great. Any problems? Okay, the next ground rule should be obvious: No name-calling, no disrespect, and no laughing at what other people say. What each person says is important, so give each other the chance to speak. And really listen to each other, too.

DEBBIE: Okay, where do you want to start?

KRISTIN: I'll start. In my neighborhood, well, I don't see many kids who are different from me. I mean, even at school—and the ones I do see always hang together. I don't think they really want to be friends with anyone else.

YVONNE: How do you know if you don't ask?

KRISTIN: But, I feel uncomfortable. I think people like to be with people who are like them—have something in common—including race.

ANDREA: That was what I was always taught by my parents and teachers—all people are basically the same. You know, it's a small world sort of thing. And, well, isn't that the way to stop people from hating each other—by talking about how people are really the same?

YVONNE: At the same time, when people emphasize the similarities, what happens to the differences?

ROBERTO: It's an easy way to ignore them!

YVONNE: Right! And how can we respect what makes people different and unique if we ignore those very things?

KRISTIN: Yeah, but, I still want to know how you can expect to value someone's differences if she doesn't want to hang around with you?

BETH ANNE: Well, no one is saying you have to like everybody. There are annoying people of all races—but, it's more of a respect thing.

DEBBIE: And taking the time to break down some stereotypes and find out what the person is really like—at the very least, not thinking that just because she is Asian, she is very smart. I get that stereotype all the time from my teachers and it is very hard. They expect me to be brilliant. And when I'm average, I almost think they're so disappointed because I don't match their expectations that I get even lower grades from them!

SHAWN: Wow—you know, I think I always kind of thought that too. And I'm embarrassed because I really know how it feels when people look at you and expect you to behave in a certain way. I'm sorry, Debbie.

DEBBIE: You're forgiven. But, I think it's harder when you're so visibly different. And, not only racially different. There's a girl in my apartment building. She's blind and has a guide dog, you know, and I always feel uncomfortable if she's leaving the building the same time as me—like, should I help her down the stairs? I open the door and then I start mumbling stuff.

YVONNE: I guess you should just ask her if she needs help and let her tell you.

BERNADETTE: Exactly! But, why do people feel so uncomfortable?

KRISTIN: Well, I think if I start by just talking to one person—one on one—maybe someone I sit next to in class or in band with me—and take it from there.

BEN: I don't know. I'm Jewish but people don't know that when they look at me. So the thing I find hard is when people start telling Jewish jokes in front of me. Then what do I do? Sometimes, I tell people, hey, I'm Jewish and then everyone gets really embarrassed and uncomfortable. And sometimes it's people I really want to get to know better and then I think I've put up a barrier. And so sometimes I just listen—but then I get so angry at myself.

BERNADETTE: You should never just listen. You have to speak up!

MAILE: That might be easy for you, Bernadette, but for some of us, it's not so easy.

LIN: You can let someone know his joke isn't funny—"Hey, putting people down isn't very funny," or "Let's be positive. Making fun of other people doesn't make me feel good."

ROBERTO: I think you have to feel comfortable about yourself—who you are—respect your own background—feel pride in it. Then it's easier to speak up.

YVONNE: My grandmother has told me stories since I was a baby about women in my family who were really strong. And I've read a couple of books. One was on queens and princesses in different African empires and another was on African-American women. Listening to my grandmother and reading those stories made me feel great inside. So, if I hear put-downs, I try hard to remember my great-great grandmother who supported her family with her own farm and managed to send two of her sons to college.

BETH ANNE: But some of us don't really identify with a particular group. My family is all mixed up, so I don't really think of myself as belonging to an ethnic group. If anyone asks me who I am, I say I'm a Southerner.

ANDREA: And really, though I have an Italian name and all, my Mom makes hamburgers more often than lasagna. And I hate when other kids think my father must be in the Mafia!

ROBERTO: That's why it's important not to stereotype people. Go back to what Debbie said. Don't expect people to act a certain way because of how they look. Like, my grandmother gets so furious when she sees older people on TV shows or in commercials shown as being helpless. She runs her own graphic design company—and she's 78!

ANDREA: And don't think someone is poor or homeless because she is lazy. There are lots of reasons for poverty or homelessness, and they're complicated.

YVONNE: So, what are the important things that we are all saying here?

ANDREA: Respect the differences among us, but also celebrate what we all have in common—like, having the freedom to even hold a forum like this one. A lot of countries don't have our freedom of speech!

LIN: Respect your own heritage. Learn more about it. And respect yourself. Feel proud of who you are—your strengths and your talents.

SHAWN: And no put-downs. Ethnic jokes aren't funny.

KRISTIN: And look beyond the stereotypes that you might learn from TV or books and magazines—or even from adults. Try to see the person inside.

BETH ANNE: And make an effort. You have to work on your own attitudes —and then work on the attitudes of others. Reach out to people.

DEBBIE: And have the courage to get beyond feeling self-conscious and make friends with people who are different. Learn more about them.

ROBERTO: Like in sports, or in debating groups, school and community clubs. Find places where different people can work together.

BERNADETTE: Like making the neighborhood better!

BEN: Exactly.

YVONNE: And when you start in your neighborhoods—well, then, you are making the world better, too. And that's a powerful feeling!

In your troop or group, discuss:

- **What ground rules did the group set? Why was this important?**

- **What problem did Kristin mention? What solution did the group develop?**

- **What advice did Lin have for dealing with put-down jokes?**

- **What were some steps the group thought would help fight prejudice?**

- **What can you do as an individual? as part of a community group?**

Prejudice & Discrimination

Prejudice means having a negative **feeling** or opinion about someone simply because of her race, ethnic background, religion, ability, or other difference. Sometimes, television, movies, and books show certain groups in an unfair way. People see these stereotypes over and over, and begin to believe them. Sometimes, people hear ethnic jokes (making fun of particular groups) or other negative remarks from their families or friends. It is hard sometimes to really keep an open mind; it is even harder to speak out or stand up for yourself or others.

Discrimination is the **action** of excluding people or treating them badly because they are seen as different. An individual, a group, an institution, or a government can practice discrimination. For example, suppose a landlord has an empty apartment he wants to rent. You call and make an appointment to go and see it. When you get there, the landlord decides that he doesn't want to rent you the apartment because of your racial, ethnic, or cultural background, or he thinks you are too old, or he thinks your disability will be a problem. So, he lies to you: "Sorry, too late, I just rented the apartment." That's discrimination. Have you ever felt discriminated against? If you haven't, can you imagine how you would feel if you really wanted to rent that apartment, and couldn't because of discrimination?

Prejudice-Busting

Remember what Roberto and Yvonne said? It is important to feel pride in yourself because studies have shown that people who have a lot of self-respect also have a lot of respect for others. Also, you might try becoming a prejudice-fighting activist. When you hear people using put-downs, tell them they are being unfair and that you don't want to listen. Also, find ways to work with people from other cultures and backgrounds: Kristin mentioned starting small by speaking to the person sitting next to you in class, and Debbie suggested having the courage to make friends with people who are different.

Working together on a project or towards a common goal helps break down stereotypes. Even if your town might not seem to have a lot of people of different cultures and ethnic backgrounds, look around your school and your community. You will be more successful if you are able to understand differing points of view and if you can help people work together.

This week I promise to fight prejudice and discrimination by

_____

_____

_____

Critical Thinking

Critical thinking means questioning things you read, see, and hear. Being able to think critically is a good skill to learn.

When you think critically you might question images, words, or other messages in the media. For example, if you used critical thinking while watching an old "western" television show and saw American Indians always shown as villains, never heroes, you might ask yourself if this is an accurate picture of American Indians. How could you find out? You could go to the library and find recent books that describe the wide variety in American Indian groups. Maybe your library or video store carries documentary videos that depict American Indian culture realistically. Perhaps you can talk to American Indians and learn about their historical perspectives. (To read about being "Media Wise," see pages 118–119.

Remember, everyone is different in her own way. Every group has good people and bad, and people who are heroes.

Stereotypes Are Everywhere

A stereotype is the belief that all the people who belong to a certain group think, act, and look the same. Stereotyping can be found almost anywhere including on television, in magazines, in books, and in the classroom. One of the best ways to put an end to stereotyped thinking is to point it out when you hear it or see it. But, first, you must be able to recognize it and figure out why it is unfair. To help recognize stereotyping, try some of the following activities:

With a group or by yourself, complete the following sentences. Try to be as honest as you can with your answers.

Girls like to _____.

Boys like to _____.

Old people are _____.

People with disabilities are _____.

Rich people like to _____.

Poor people like to _____.

Fat people are _____.

Foreigners are _____.

Kids who get straight As are _____.

People who speak other languages are _____.

Think about your answers. Are they always true? Why or why not? Using the sentences above as a guide, talk about how stereotypes are harmful.

Page through books and magazines, or scan television programs to find stereotypes. An example might be an advertisement for a new computer game that shows a boy thinking about his next move with a girl looking over his shoulder. This may suggest that only boys are good at computer games or that girls don't enjoy working on a computer. Choose an example and show how you would break the stereotype.

Other Kinds of Prejudice and Discrimination

▲ Last night, Mr. Hawkins, the high school assistant principal, awoke in the middle of the night to the smell of smoke. The smoke was coming from the front of his home. He ran to the window and saw a cross burning on his front lawn.

▲ Melissa returned home from school in tears. Her mother gave her a big hug and asked her what was wrong. In a sobbing voice, Melissa told her mother that her friends said she was too fat to try out for the cheerleading squad.

▲ Alicia thought she was being punished. Why else would her teacher, Mr. Stevens, ask her to be science-project partners with Anthony? After all, Alicia was the most popular kid in the class and Anthony—well, Anthony had no friends, wore clothes two sizes too small, and smelled. She knew she would just die if anyone saw her talking to him.

Which of the above shows prejudice and discrimination?

That's right, all of them do. Prejudice doesn't always involve race, religion, or ethnic background. Some people may be prejudiced against others who don't dress like the popular group at school or against people who don't play sports well. Feelings of prejudice can be directed toward people who are homeless or are super-smart or wear hearing aids or use food stamps. Prejudice can be directed against a person's appearance, sexual orientation, class in society, age, or almost any part of the person that makes her different.

Have you ever been hurt by prejudice and discrimination? If so, how did it make you feel? What did you do about it?

Words Can Sometimes Hurt

"Is it okay if I sit here?" Maria asked quietly.

"Ummm, sure," said Allison without looking up.

Maria set her lunch tray down and slid in on the bench next to Kathy. She heard someone giggle at the other end of the table.

"Would anybody like to play baseball after school today?" asked Kathy.

"All right," said Allison. "Hey, Maria, would you like to come?"

Maria quickly looked up. "I would love…" Splat! The pizza slid right off the plate! Maria jumped up. "I'm sorry, Kathy…it was an accident…I didn't mean…"

Kathy started screaming before she could even finish. "Oh, Maria! You're such a jerk! How could you be so stupid? Forget it–you're not playing baseball with us today 'cause you're too big a loser!"

How would you feel if you were Maria? If you were Allison, what would you say to Maria? to Kathy?

Pretend you are sitting at the other end of this lunch table and had just witnessed this whole event. You are friends with both Maria and Kathy and are looking forward to the baseball game after school today. Continue the story telling how you would stop your friends from fighting. Go back to page 57 for tips on conflict-resolution skills.

Name-calling is very hurtful. Not only is it hurtful but it can lead others to form stereotypes. Some people tend to group others into categories because it is easier than really getting to know them. But this is an unfair way of looking at people because you never really get to know the individual.

For example, other kids who don't know Maria and heard what Kathy said may think Maria isn't smart or a good athlete and never ask her to be a part of a school project or sports team. And, if they believe Maria isn't a good athlete or student, they may put her close friends in the same categories. They, too, become "stupid" and "losers."

The Generation at the Top: Senior Citizens

"Hey, Miranda, where's Deborah? Is she coming to the movie with us?" asked Darcy.

"I called her to see if she wanted to go but she said she was going to her grandmother's house for dinner," replied Miranda. "I'm not really sure why."

"What d'ya mean?" asked Darcy.

"Well," said Miranda, "how much fun can that be? My grandfather never has much to say and goes to bed really early."

"Hmmm...you're kinda right. Now that I think about it, old people are pretty boring," Darcy said.

Senior citizens are another group of people hurt by stereotypes. Miranda's and Darcy's feelings show what many people have been led to believe about older people. Have you ever taken the time to get to know an older person? What did you discover?

Many older people have a great deal to share. In addition to talents and abilities, many senior citizens are involved in learning new skills and hobbies, earning a college degree, and beginning new careers. Older people are as diverse as young people in their talents, skills, and abilities. Try some of these activities to find out more about senior citizens:

 Invite senior citizens to be speakers, chaperones, and guests at your Girl Scout activities and events.

 Study how older people are portrayed on television programs, in movies, and in books. Are they represented as a diverse group of individuals or do they seem to be of the same type? What changes would you make to break the stereotypes?

 Find out more about the special joys and problems of growing old by talking to relatives or neighbors.

 Ask a senior citizen to share her knowledge of a subject or activity that interests you, such as a foreign language, gardening, art, travel, or local history.

People with Disabilities

Another group of people who have been hurt by stereotypes are people with disabilities. A person with a disability is not able to do certain things. A person who is blind cannot see and someone who is

hearing impaired has less than perfect hearing. Although these individuals may have other abilities and talents, some people focus only on what people with disabilities can't do and not what they can do.

Sarah is blind and reads by using Braille, a special type of printing in which raised dots are felt by the fingers. Sarah can sing in a chorus, play games, solve math problems, and do all other things that do not require vision. Nancy uses special crutches to get around. She can write stories on her computer, cook a meal, and play video games with her friends.

Since 1912, many Girl Scouts with and without disabilities have worked together on learning and practicing camping skills, doing service projects, and completing badge requirements. Try some of the following activities:

 Do a survey of your meeting place to find out how accessible it is for people with disabilities. Measure the doorways and bathroom facilities to find out if they are accessible to someone in a wheelchair. Think of ways to get rid of any obstacles.

 Read more about people with disabilities like Ryan White, Stevie Wonder, Amelia Earhart, Agatha Christie, Marlee Matlin, Albert Einstein, or Juliette Gordon Low. Why are they famous?

 Experience the feelings and frustrations of having a disability. Put mittens on your hands or tape your fingers together and try to button your shirt or tie your shoe. Tune in to your favorite television program but turn the volume all the way down. How did you feel when you tried these activities? What reactions did you notice or receive from other people? Did you ask for or require assistance? Share your feelings with other members of your troop or family.

 Find out what services are available for people with disabilities in your neighborhood or community. Invite someone who works with people with disabilities to speak to your troop or group.

 Study the finger-spellling sign language alphabet on the next page. Learn to sign your name and say "hello," "I am a Girl Scout," "please," "thank you," and "goodbye."

Learning to Respect Differences

 Be a heritage investigator! What can you learn about people who share your heritage? Look for someone in your family's past who made a contribution or had qualities that you admire. Look for role models today in your community and beyond. Think of ways you can share what you have discovered with the girls in your troop or group or younger girls.

 Try to discover all you can about the contributions of groups different from your own. Look around your community, county, or state. What can you discover?

 To help stop stereotyping, try creating a "contract" that would make certain behaviors unacceptable. For example, "No ethnic jokes. If I hear an ethnic joke, I'll tell the person to stop." Try to get three people to sign the contract.

Plan a "Prejudice-Free Day" in your community or school. Look at the action-plan steps on pages 141–142 for help in getting started. Why not try activities from Celebrating People, Creative Solutions, or The World in My Community badges.

 What does the Girl Scout Promise and Law state about the ways you should treat other people? How can you put what it says into action?

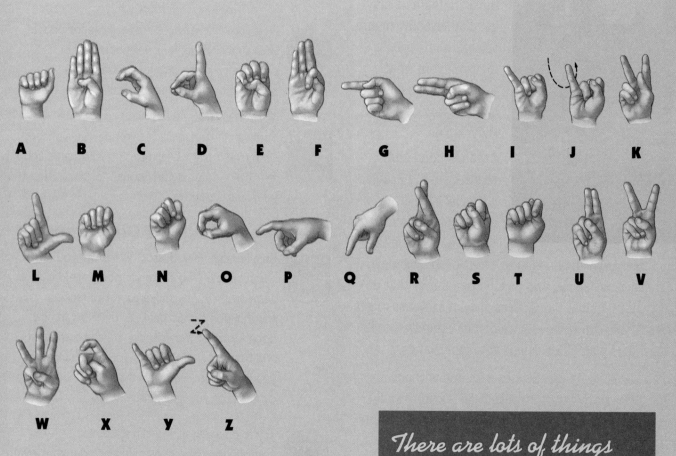

Finger-Spelling Sign Language Alphabet

There are lots of things you can do. You have the power to make changes. You have the power to help people learn to live and work together. It starts with you. What are your ideas?

LEADERSHIP IN ACTION

CHAPTER 6

What Skills Do Leaders Have?

Leadership Hall of Fame

Girls Can Do It

Your Own Leadership Action Project

May Peace Prevail on Earth

Reine sólo la Paz en la Tierra

Leadership, which can take many forms and styles, is an important part of Girl Scouting. This chapter will help you identify your own leadership style. Have you thought about how to channel your ideas into a neighborhood project? Why not use the information on leadership action projects to help you get started?

Leaders have:
- Creativity
- Ideas about how things might be
- Determination
- Commitment
- A sense of humor
- Enthusiasm
- Respect for others
- Fair-mindedness
- An ability to keep organized

So they can:
- Help the group set goals, make decisions, evaluate progress
- Plan
- Find solutions
- Guide and direct
- Organize
- Help others cooperate
- Teach
- Support
- Empower
- Keep the peace
- Keep track of time
- Take risks
- Inspire
- Keep the group focused
- Help others develop their leadership skills

What Is Leadership?

Leadership: to show the way; to guide or cause others to follow you; to direct; to be in charge.

Who are your leaders? Think of people you know and some you don't know. Did you think of the President of the U.S.A. or your Girl Scout leader? You can often identify a leader in a group by the way she acts, or the way others act towards her.

List some leaders. Include leaders in school, community, state, nation, and the world. Pick your favorite leader from the list. Share with someone why you think that person is a leader.

_____

_____

_____

_____

_____

_____

_____

Leadership Style

Juliette Gordon Low was a memorable leader. She loved what she was doing, and one reason that girls and adults followed her was because she communicated her enthusiasm. She also was known for her ability to begin something, then step back and let others take over, once she was sure they were on the right track.

Leadership doesn't depend on being Ms. Perfect or Ms. Right-All-the-Time. Most people who have leadership experience tell stories about things that have gone wrong when they were leading a group. But they will also tell you what they learned from their mistakes.

Part of being a good leader is helping others feel good about their work. That means choosing the right person for the right job and encouraging others when they are doing something new. People always like to feel that what they are doing is important to the group effort.

Here are some common leadership styles. Which ones best match your skills and abilities?

Director: Gives very good direction and makes sure everyone does her or his job. She will make certain that rules are clear and that everyone is expected to follow them.

Coach: Uses a style that provides both direction and supervision but encourages the involvement of everyone! She will explain the work that lies ahead, discuss decisions, and answer questions.

Supporter: Works with other members of a group to set goals and list steps to achieve those goals. She encourages everyone to make decisions and gives each member the help they need.

Delegator: Gives everyone a share of the work. She lets group members make decisions and take as much responsibility as they can handle. She is there to answer questions, but she wants them to take as much responsibility for their actions as possible.

List all of the ways you are a leader. Decide on some skills or abilities that leaders have that you would like to develop in yourself. Come up with a plan for becoming a better leader and then do the following: Take on a leadership role for three months in your troop, school, or community. Be a leader for a sports team, an art project, a music group, or a computer network. Or, organize a neighborhood service club. Keep a journal of your time spent as a leader.

Girls Can Do It

Quick, close your eyes and think of three people you consider to be leaders. Did you list any women leaders? Good for you if you did! A lot of people would not.

 Ask others to name some leaders. (Ask a variety of people.) Compare the answers that you get. Do answers vary from male to female? Does a person's age make a difference? Share your surveys in your group or troop.

When Juliette Gordon Low was a leader, it was not common for women to assume leadership beyond the family. Nor was it common for a deaf person to lead others.

Today, some people still believe that women and kids can't be leaders.

Here are some "Can't Do" statements you might encounter along your path to leadership:

• Girls take forever to decide on anything.

• Girls can't go camping—because they're afraid of bugs.

• Girls can't be leaders because they're not as strong as boys.

• You're just a kid; why should I listen to you?

What are some other "Can't Do" statements you have heard? Discuss how statements like these can put up "roadblocks" for girls. One way to leap over roadblocks is to use critical thinking skills. (See page 126).

Another way to achieve goals is to seek the help of a mentor, an older girl or woman in a leadership position who is willing to advise you. A mentor could be your troop or group leader, a teacher or a member of your family.

Note: There are certain things you cannot do while representing Girl Scouts because it is a nonprofit organization. Endorsing products or candidates, lobbying lawmakers, collecting money for other organizations, or asking for donations are some examples. Your leader will help you determine what can be done; you and your leader can use *Safety-Wise* as a guide.

You can learn how to do all of these things and put the leadership training you gain from Girl Scouts to use in community and school actions.

 Here are some situations that require leadership. Discuss which styles could be used with each situation. You might even want to practice each style with friends. Remember, there is no right or wrong answer.

• You have a large group. The job is to plan three activities for a Girl Scout camporee.

• You and five other girls have been asked to plan a flag ceremony for a councilwide event.

• You are leading a hike when you spot a tornado in the distance.

Leadership Hall of Fame

The girls in this fictional Leadership Hall of Fame represent leadership in action. One of them may remind you of someone you know, or may be you in a few years. Being a Girl Scout is a great place to learn and practice leadership. You can celebrate your successes with friends and learn from your mistakes. Listen to what the Hall of Famers have to say about their leadership projects. See if you can pick out some characteristics they share as leaders.

Name: Maggie Rodriguez

From: California, U.S.A.

Claim to fame: Started a school recycling program with her Cadette Girl Scout troop. Received her Girl Scout Silver Award.

Highlights: After deciding that they wanted to do something about the waste at school, Maggie's troop got permission to start a trial recycling program. Each troop member was responsible for a different job: setting up the recycling in the cafeteria, and classroom, creating an education campaign, and organizing a recycling dance!

Maggie worked with the cafeteria manager to set up recycling of food, paper, and plastic utensils. The project was so successful that the school district adopted a full-time recycling program.

Comments about leadership: "This was definitely a team effort! Each of us was responsible for putting together our own committee. We rotated leadership of the meeting each week to make sure everyone had a chance to contribute. At one of our meetings, we had a woman, who is president of her company, come speak about working with groups. We had a lot of questions about the way some of our committees were working together and she really helped us."

Problems: "The hardest part was getting all of the students to cooperate at first. We ended up making some goofy awards for people who were not recycling. They were great sports, and when they decided to join us, their friends did, too."

Name: Sandi Baker

From: New York, U.S.A.

Claim to fame: Volunteer tutor at a homeless shelter.

Highlights: Sandi, a sixth-grader, was trained to tutor children through a program at her public library. After working on her Women Today badge, Sandi saw the need for tutoring kids at a community shelter. She worked with the shelter director to begin a program. Sandi involved her school, her community, and people at the shelter to create a children's recreation and study area.

Comments about leadership: "I didn't start out to be a leader. I just got tired of everybody talking about the homeless and not doing anything. I learned I could make things change by getting others to work with me on a goal. I also learned that it is important to involve the people you are helping. The residents now have a say in the running of their shelter. That's empowerment!"

Problems: "At first I thought that because people didn't do anything, they didn't want to get involved. I found that people needed to be asked. And I learned how to ask for help. There was no way I could build bookcases for the books we collected. So I asked some girls and boys in the shop class at school. Now they are building a playhouse for the kids."

Name: Emily Mabaya

From: Kenya

Claim to fame: A member of the Green Belt Movement, an organization that plants trees and gardens to fight soil erosion and deforestation in her country.

Highlights: After becoming a member of the Green Belt Movement, Emily saw the interest other women had whenever she talked about her efforts. So she started talking to others about the organization and showed them how to plant. Women from the next village came to see how they did it. Soon, she was talking to groups about the Green Belt Movement.

Comments about leadership: "I always thought of myself as a quiet person. But because I want my children to grow strong and healthy in this land and I feel strongly about what we're doing, I could talk easily to others. Bit by bit, I feel, we will make our country green."

Problems: "It was hard to make people understand how important trees and gardens are. I know many people thought I was foolish. But once women saw how much money they could make selling the vegetables in the market, they did not think I was so foolish. And I know how much these gardens help the environment."

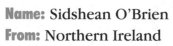

Name: Sidshean O'Brien

From: Northern Ireland

Claim to fame: Meets once a week with children of Protestant and Catholic groups to play games and share friendship.

Highlights: Sidshean's mother began working with a movement to bring Protestant and Catholic women together to promote peace in Belfast. Sidshean organizes games and activities that she thinks the children will like. She's discovered that all children, despite their differences, like to have fun, laugh, and make friends.

Comments about leadership: "Sometimes leadership means taking a very small step. We can't stop the fighting that happens in our country, but we can bring groups of children together to learn about each other. If everyone took a small step, maybe the fighting and hatred would lessen."

Problems: "What we are doing with the children makes some people very angry. But I know there are other people who support the peace movement and that my mother and the other adults know what is right. They tell me it's important to act on one's beliefs."

It's up to you: What does it mean to be a peacemaker? What are the risks involved? What are the rewards? Design a way to express what the world would be like at peace. Or, make a peace pole, with the word "Peace," or the phrase "May Peace Prevail on Earth" written on four sides of a pole (See the next page for a sample peace pole.) Place the pole where people can reflect on what peace means, like in a public garden or at camp. Here are some ways of saying peace in different languages:

AMAMI	SWAHILI
FRIEDEN	GERMAN
HEIWA	JAPANESE
HEPING	MANDARIN
MIR	RUSSIAN
PAIX	FRENCH
SALAAM	ARABIC
SHALOM	HEBREW
WOKIYAPI	SIOUX
PAZ	SPANISH

Name: Kimberly Ting

From: Texas, U.S.A.

Claim to fame: Girl assistant troop leader. Helps lead a Brownie Girl Scout troop.

Highlights: Kim has always enjoyed working with younger children. This began when she earned her Caring for Children badge as a Junior Girl Scout and became a program aide at day camp. Last year, as a Senior Girl Scout, she completed her Leader-in-Training project under an experienced Brownie Girl Scout leader. This year she is paired with Mrs. Papadopolous, a new leader in her neighborhood, and together they lead a Brownie Girl Scout troop.

Comments about leadership: "I learned so much from my mentor leader last year! She let me try a lot of new things with the girls. And not everything worked...like the time a guest speaker didn't show and I didn't have a plan for what to do, or the time I led everyone down the wrong trail and had to ask directions from a ranger. But you know, I learned more from the mistakes than the things that went really well. And so did the girls. Probably the most important thing I learned was how to give others the chance to make decisions."

Problems: "It was hard at first working with Mrs. Papadopolous because she was so new to Girl Scouting. I knew more about the activities than she did. But I learned that Mrs. Papadopolous knew a lot about how to organize and get parents involved. Now, we're really working as a team."

Peace poles are four-sided wooden pillars inscribed with the words "May Peace Prevail on Earth" in at least four different languages. They have been placed all over the world to remind people to think about peace.

MAKING CHANGES IN YOUR COMMUNITY

You are a citizen of the world, your country, your state, and your community. As a citizen, you have rights and responsibilities. For example, you have the right to use a public park and the responsibility to let others enjoy it too by not littering or disturbing others with a loud radio. When you do things like recycle, conserve water, vote in a school election, or do a service project, you are acting as a responsible citizen.

Active Citizenship

Active citizens care for and improve the place they live. Sometimes it's easier not to act. For example, if the corner trash can is full, it is easier to throw a candy wrapper on the ground than walk another block to find an empty trash can, or write the sanitation department and ask them to empty the trash cans more often. But, if all your neighbors throw their trash on the ground, your community becomes dirty and unpleasant. This is why citizens need to act to identify and solve community problems. Take a look at the chart on the following page. It includes problems and actions to solve them. Do any of these problems look familiar?

Place	Issue	Action
School	The cafeteria is not set up for recycling	• Form a student/adult advisory committee. • Talk to a member of the parent/teacher's association. • Make a presentation to the school board.
Neighborhood	There is an increase in burglaries	• Form a group and talk to neighborhood residents. • Schedule a meeting with the police department. • Set up a "neighborhood watch" program and distribute stickers.
Larger Community	There is a lack of services for senior citizens and children	• Make a pamphlet of community services for senior citizens and children. • Ask your Girl Scout council for help with getting pamphlets printed. • Distribute pamphlets to senior citizens and parents at shopping centers.
Environment	A severe winter storm eroded the park's soil	• Contact county parks department about problem. • Organize volunteers for a "planting day" event. • Plant shrubs on hillside.

Where do you start when you want to be part of or begin a project? Each girl profiled in this chapter had a reason for starting or joining in a project. Most of the projects started as someone's vision of something that was needed, whether it was at school or in the community.

Although the projects were different, they shared some basic steps in becoming a finished project. If you have an idea for a project or want to come up with an idea for a project, consider these steps:

CREATING A LEADERSHIP ACTION PROJECT

1. Brainstorm possibilities with your troop or group.

Maggie's troop (see page 135) decided that waste was a problem at their school. They listed all the things they might do to make others aware of the problem:

- Make posters
- Have an art contest with recycled materials
- Recycle paper in class
- Circulate a petition
- Make recycling bins
- Talk to the cafeteria manager
- Talk to the recycling depot
- Talk to the principal
- Start recycling

2. Make decisions.

Maggie's troop members narrowed their list after discussion. They decided that talking to the principal was a friendlier approach than circulating a petition. They knew their project would take little money because they planned to use recycled materials. The big

question was whether they could get the paper and plastics picked up by the recycling company or sanitation department. That was resolved when someone talked to the woman in charge.

3. Plan your calendar.

Several dates were chosen by Maggie's group. The dates needed to be checked out with the principal. The dance date needed to be cleared by the student activities group. Meetings were set up with the principal and the head of the recycling depot. It was decided that troop or group meeting dates would work for committee meetings.

4. Put your ideas into action.

Once the plans were outlined, Maggie's troop divided up the jobs. A committee was formed to complete each task. Committee heads met once a week to make sure they were on track before the big event.

5. Evaluate what was done.

One week after the event, Maggie's troop completed an evaluation. Each person told what she had learned, what she would change, and what she liked most about the project. The troop also wrote a report for their principal outlining what they had done and why. The principal used the report when it came time to describe the project to the school board.

6. Share your success.

After the successful project, the girls in Maggie's troop threw an ice cream party for committee members. Everyone got great buttons that came from the recycling depot. Maggie and her committee heads wrote thank-you notes to the cafeteria manager, principal, and the head of the recycling depot.

YOUR OWN ACTION PLAN

Create your own action plan for a community project. Use the following action plan outline.

1

Brainstorm ideas. These are the ideas that we brainstormed:

1._____

_____

2._____

_____

3._____

_____

4._____

_____

This is the idea we chose:

_____

_____

_____

2

Make decisions.

Information we need to get:

_____

_____

This is what the plan will cost:

_____

_____

We can get materials from:

_____

We can get help from:

_____

_____

Special permission will be obtained from:

_____

_____

Our troop or group voted that:

_____

_____

3

Plan your calendar.

We need to meet with:

_____

on _____
        (date)

We also need to meet with:

_____

on _____
        (date)

We need to meet on: _____
                (date)

Our date to finish is: _____
                (date)

4

Put your ideas into action.

_____

(name of person or committee)

will work on _____

_____

(name of person or committee)

will work on _____

_____

_____

(name of person or committee)

will work on _____

143

5

Evaluate what was done.

What we liked about the project:

_____
_____
_____
_____
_____

What we would do differently:

_____
_____
_____
_____

We would do it/not do it again because:
(circle one)

_____
_____
_____
_____

6

We need to send thank-you notes to:

_____
_____
_____

We will celebrate our success by:

_____
_____
_____

on:_____
(date)

We will tell our Girl Scout council and
_____about our success.
(other people or groups)

 Now is the time to try your wings and fly with a leadership-in-action project. Focus on what you would like to do and work through the six steps of leadership in action while doing an actual project. Keep a journal to help you evaluate. If you do this as a troop or a group, make sure that each person has the opportunity to lead within the group.

As you can see, leadership can take many forms. And as a leader, you need to find your own style—one that feels comfortable and still helps you arrive at your goals. Remember that your troop or group members and Girl Scout leader are there to help you discover your unique way of leading.

EXPLORING INTERESTS, SKILLS, & TALENTS

Playing and Watching Sports

Optical Illusions: What Do You See?

Study Bubbleology!

Skills for Outdoor Adventures

One of the best things about Girl Scouting is that it offers you lots of ideas for fun things to do. And, *you* get to decide the activities. In this chapter, you'll find many activities—for all interests, skills, and talents—to do alone or with your troop or group.

Some of the activities will have a safety symbol near them. This is to remind you to be extra careful in doing the activity or to ask an adult to assist you.

What do you do when you feel bored?

One of the great things about being a Girl Scout is that you have a group of friends with whom you can explore interests, skills, and talents! You don't have to worry about making a fool of yourself the first time you in-line skate because you have a friend cheering you on (or one who's fallen on the ground with you!).

Not everyone in your troop or group will be interested in exploring the same things. But you will probably find some girls who share your interest.

PLAYING SPORTS AND GAMES

Playing sports, either alone or with others, is a great way to have fun. No matter which sport you choose, you will need to learn certain skills and follow certain rules. Remember always to play fairly and do your best. To get started, you may want to try the Sports badge or the Sports Sampler badge in *Girl Scout Badges and Signs.*

TIPS FOR PLAYING SPORTS

☆ Always do warm-up exercises before taking part in a sports activity, and always do cool-down exercises afterwards.

☆ Wear clothing and shoes that are comfortable and suitable for the sport you are playing.

☆ Use equipment that is in good condition.

☆ Practice or play in an area that is safe and free of hazards.

☆ Drink water before you start and often during your exercise.

☆ Stop playing if you get hurt or feel tired.

TIPS FOR WATCHING SPORTS

Watching sports can also be fun. You can become an expert on a sport by learning all you can about it, even if you don't play. Here are some rules for being a good spectator or fan.

☆ Stay in the viewing area and away from the playing area at all times.

☆ Be quiet if players need to concentrate or listen, even if they are on the other team.

☆ Support players when they do well, but do not criticize when they make a mistake.

☆ Make sure you do not interfere with the enjoyment of other fans.

The sports described here are just a few you can try. See what others you can find out about.

SOFTBALL

Softball is like baseball in many ways, but there are a few differences. A softball is larger and weighs less, and the bat is also larger and lighter than the one used for baseball. Slow-pitch softball, which most people play, usually has two teams of ten players each.

Softball games may last either seven or nine innings, depending on the league rules. Each team gets three outs in their turn at-bat.

◆ Throwing

If you are right-handed, you will step forward with your left foot as you throw. If you are left-handed, you step with your right foot. Lean your body backwards as you use your arm.

◆ Pitching

In slow-pitch softball, all pitching is done underhanded. The ball should arc on its way to the plate.

◆ Catching

The most important thing to remember is always to keep your eyes on the ball. To "get under" the ball, keep your arms extended and your hands relaxed. When the ball hits your glove, let your arms and hands "give" a little.

◆ Batting

It sometimes takes practice to learn how to hit the ball, but once you learn how to stand comfortably, you will find hitting easier. If you are right-handed, you will stand with the plate to your right. If you are left-handed, it will be to your left.

BASKETBALL

Basketball is a team sport played with a ball and basket, usually on a court. It is a fast-paced game that involves running, dribbling, passing, and shooting.

Playing the Game

Regulation basketball is played on a court with one basket at each end. The two teams are made up of five players each. Points are scored by shooting the ball into the basket the other team is defending. A team gets two points for every successful basket shot. But, if a player has violated a rule (such as tripping a player), the other team is given a foul shot. A foul shot is made from the free-throw line. One point is earned for a successful throw.

Players move the ball by dribbling it or passing it to members of their team. If a team member "travels," walks or runs with the ball without dribbling, she will lose possession of the ball to the other team.

You can learn a lot about the specific rules and strategies by watching a game.

Techniques

Learn and practice these skills:

- Dribble (bounce) the ball while running and standing still.

- Pass a ball to another player in these three ways: a chest pass (with two hands), an overhead pass, and a bounce.

- Shoot a ball into a basket in these ways: a set shot, a jump shot, and a lay-up. For the set shot and the jump shot, use either one or two hands. Shoot the lay-up with two hands.

- Guard a player who has the ball.

Variations of the Game

If you don't have ten players or a regulation court—or if you want to try something different—you can play variations of the game. For example, you can:

- Play a game with two, three, or four players on a team.

- Play with only one hoop.

- Change the rules so that only passing, no dribbling, is allowed.

SOCCER

The object of soccer is to kick the soccer ball into your opponent's goal. It involves a lot of running, kicking, blocking, and dribbling. Soccer is played by two teams with a maximum of 11 players on each team. A soccer game has two periods. A good soccer player develops balance and timing, which come from practicing soccer skills.

◆ Kicking

To learn to kick well, practice from a standing position first. Keep your head down and your eyes on the ball. Put your non-kicking foot next to the ball. Use the instep (inside) of your foot to kick. After you kick the ball, keep moving your kicking leg forward (this is called follow-through). When you are comfortable with kicking this way, practice with others while the ball is rolling or bouncing.

◆ Blocking

There are three major kinds of blocks. In the "body block," bend your back slightly as the ball hits your body so the ball won't bounce wildly. "Heading" is a type of block where the player controls the ball to clear, pass, or score by hitting it with the top of the forehead. In "trapping," you stop the ball with the inside or outside of your shoe or with the sole of your foot.

◆ Dribbling

Dribbling is one way to move the soccer ball forward. You do this by giving the ball short kicks with the inside or outside of your foot. At the same time, you try to keep your opponent from taking the ball.

MORE ABOUT SPORTS

There are other sports you and your friends in Girl Scouting may want to try. Swimming, field hockey, archery, tennis, and bicycling are just a few. Your school or local library may have some information about these sports, or a local recreation agency may be able to help you. You might also find ideas from such badges as Hiker, Horse Lover, Horseback Rider, Swimming, and Walking for Fitness in Girl Scout Badges and Signs. Remember, you don't have to be perfect at sports, you just have to find a sport you like and have fun!

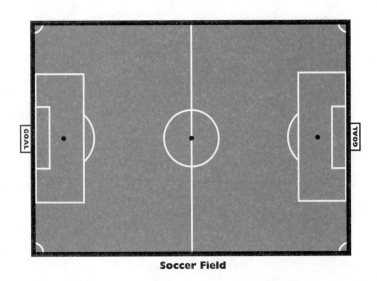

Soccer Field

Exploring the Arts

Arts activities help bring out your creativity. Don't be afraid to try something new. You might find you have a new talent just waiting to come out!

Music

Here are different kinds of music. Find out something about each of them and share your knowledge with your troop or group. If you play an instrument, you might want to play to demonstrate one of these styles of music.

- Swing
- Rock
- Pop
- Jazz
- Cajun
- Reggae
- Broadway show tunes
- Symphonic
- Country and Western
- Rap
- Salsa
- Bluegrass

Singing

Look at the music categories above and choose a song you want to sing or teach. Or, compose your own song using the blank music sheet. For more ideas, look at the Musician and Music Lover badges in *Girl Scout Badges and Signs*.

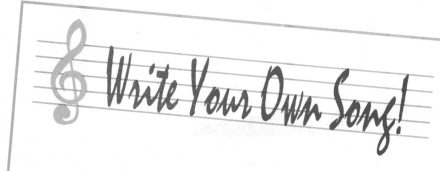

Write Your Own Song!

Drawing and Painting

Drawing

Some tools for drawing are pencil, pen, chalk, pastels, and charcoal. You can find out about each of these at an art-supply store. You can also learn about artists' supplies from an art teacher.

Painting

 Instead of painting with a brush, why not try painting with sponges, cotton swabs, bird feathers, or twigs? Choose one of these to paint a story or make your own design.

Scratchboard

 Try this variation of a scratch board, a form of drawing in which, instead of pencil or ink lines being added to white paper, a covering of color is scratched away with a pin to form a design.

CAUTION!

You Will Need:
- **Heavy, smooth white paper**
- **Colored crayons**
- **Black crayons**
- **A large safety pin or metal nail file**

1. Cover different areas of the paper with different colors of crayon.

2. Color over the entire paper with the black crayon, pressing hard.

3. When the entire paper is covered, scratch away your design. (It's best to do this over layers of newspaper, as the scraped crayon can make a mess.)

Decoupage

Decoupage is a means of decorating with paper cutouts. Originally, decoupage artists cut out paper designs and glued them to furniture. When the furniture was varnished or lacquered, it looked as if the designs had been painted on.

You can use pictures cut out from magazines, postcards, greeting cards, wrapping paper, or photographs for decorating with this technique.

Decoupage for a Planter

You Will Need:

- **A clean soup can**
- **Paint**
- **A paintbrush**
- **A cup of water**
- **Paper towels**
- **Pictures or decal stickers**
- **Varnish**
- **Potting soil**
- **Gravel (or pebbles and seeds)**

1. Peel the label off the empty can.

2. Paint all around the can and let it dry.

3. Wash the brush; then dry it.

4. Glue pictures on the can.

5. Varnish the entire can. Let it dry. Varnish again and allow it to dry completely.

6. Put gravel in the bottom of the can, and then add some soil. Carefully put your plant into the planter, and fill the sides and bottom of the planter with soil.

Optical Illusions

Hidden Picture

A picture mysteriously appears on a sheet of blank paper. You won't believe your eyes!

You Will Need:
- **White construction paper**
- **Colored paints or crayons**

Draw anything you like on a sheet of paper following these three rules:

1. The colors must be strong and solid with no shading.

2. The design must be no bigger than 3"– 6" (8 –15 cm) across (see example below).

3. Avoid small, intricate color patterns.

Put a dot in the center of your design to control the movement of your eyes. Stare at the center dot for 30 seconds. Don't move your eyes around. Keep them open wide. After 30 seconds, quickly stare at a blank sheet of white paper. Wait several seconds. What do you see?

The design you see is called an after-image. Did you notice that the colors in the after-image were different from the colors in your original design? You are seeing each color's complementary color. The basic complementary colors are:

Red–green   yellow-**purple**

blue–orange   **black**–white

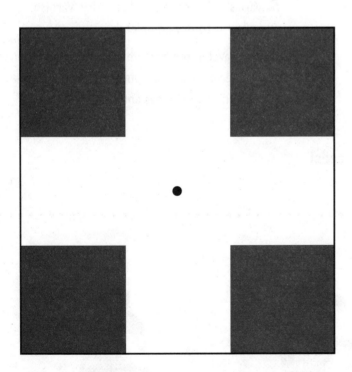

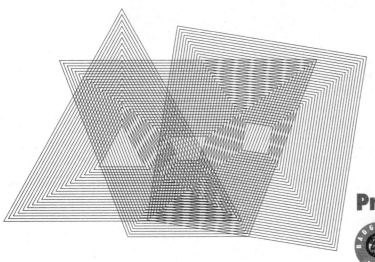

Mathematical Moiré

Can you draw straight lines that appear to be curvy?

You Will Need:
- A pen
- A ruler
- A compass for making circles
- Sheets of tracing paper

1. In the center of a piece of tracing paper, construct a small (1/2" or 13 mm) triangle, circle, square, or other geometric figure. Use a ruler for straight-line figures and a compass for circles.

2. Carefully draw the same figure outside the original, keeping lines parallel and as close as possible without touching. A space of 1/8" or 1/4 cm is good, 1/16" or 1/8 cm is even better.

3. Draw larger figures until half the page is full.

4. Repeat the same process on a different sheet of paper. You can make the same design or a different one.

5. Place one design over the other and move the sheets around. What happens to the straight lines?

For a variation, try making patterns with string art. Tap small nails into a wooden board. (Read about tools on page 103.) Then lace fine string or thread around the nails to make patterns that seem to curve and wave.

Printmaking

You can make prints in many ways. The Prints and Graphics badge in *Girl Scout Badges and Signs* has several ideas you can try. Here is one for stenciling:

You Will Need:
- **Wax paper or other nonabsorbent paper**
- **A scissors**
- **A piece of sponge**
- **Water-based paint or ink**
- **A bowl**
- **Blank cards or paper**

1. Cover your work surface with newspapers.

2. Draw your design on the wax paper.

3. Cut out the stencil design. You will use what remains on the paper as your stencil.

4. Pour the ink into the bowl.

5. Dip the sponge into the ink.

6. Press the stencil over the card or paper. Dab the sponge over the stencil to make a print. Be careful not to have too much ink or paint on the sponge. Tap off the excess onto newspaper. You may want to make your own greeting cards or wrapping paper.

Sculpture

Plaster, clay, wood, paper, and even ice are some of the things used to make sculpture. By carving, modeling, or gluing things together, you can make sculptures. One type of sculpture is given here; you can find more activities in the Ceramics and Clay badge in *Girl Scout Badges and Signs*.

Carving

A way to make sculpture is to mix plaster of paris and vermiculite. This mixture makes an easy-to-carve soft material, but looks like stone when you finish.

You Will Need:
- **Plaster of paris**
- **Vermiculite (available in hardware stores or garden centers)**
- **A bucket with water for mixing**
- **Rags for cleaning**
- **Newspapers for a work surface**
- **A stick for stirring**
- **Cardboard milk containers**
- **A small kitchen knife**

1. Fill the bucket about half-full of water to make several sculpture forms. Mix the plaster of paris in the bucket by tossing handfuls of plaster into the water until small mounds form. Stir. The mixture should be slightly thick.

2. Add about as much vermiculite as you did plaster of paris, and stir until everything is well mixed. Be careful not to pour this mixture down a drain, as it can cause clogging..

3. Pour the mixture into the milk containers. Stir once to get rid of bubbles.

4. Let the containers set either several hours in bright sunlight or overnight. When the mixture has hardened, peel off the cardboard container.

5. Use the knife to chip or carve away pieces to make a figure or design.

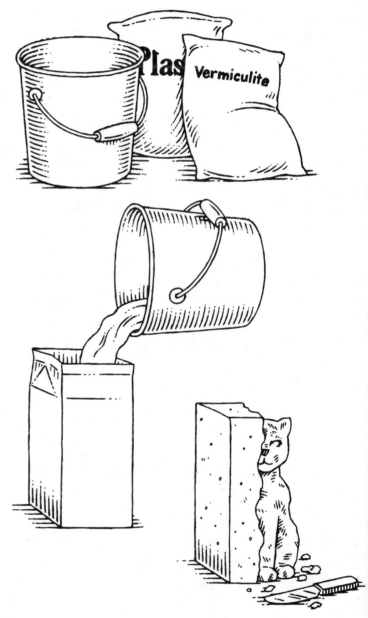

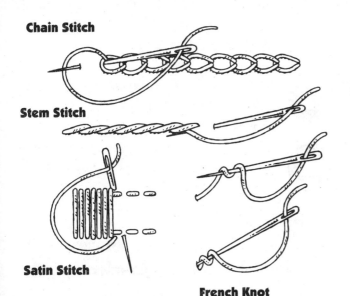

Chain Stitch

Stem Stitch

Satin Stitch

French Knot

Embroidery

You can use embroidery thread and needles to decorate your jeans, a jacket, a cloth purse, or a wall hanging. The basic stitches you will need are the chain stitch, the stem stitch, the satin stitch, and the French knot. Why not combine different stitches to decorate an item you choose?

Jewelry Making

You can use many different materials—clay, papier-mâché, bread dough, metal, wire, wood, paper—to make your own jewelry. Here are two jewelry-making ideas.

Beadwork

Use beads to make jewelry. Collect beads from craft stores, or you can make your own from clay, papier-mâché, or even paper. You might also want to try gluing beads onto T-shirts, hats, or fabric purses to make one-of-a-kind designs. Here is one type of beadwork to make necklaces, bracelets, or rings. Be sure to use a strong thread, like nylon.

Beaded Bracelet

1. Push two threaded needles (one at a time) through the first three beads.

2. Then use one needle to thread one more bead and the other needle to thread the other bead.

3. Push the two needles through one more bead.

4. Then use one needle to thread three beads and the other needle to thread three other beads.

5. Push one needle up through six beads and the other needle down through six beads.

6. Thread the number of beads you want in your design.

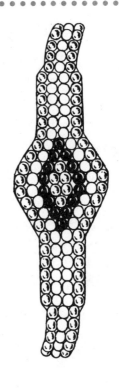

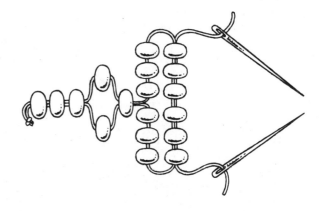

Knotted Necklaces and Bracelets

You can make necklaces with lightweight cord or friendship bracelets with embroidery thread. (See the section on knots, pages 185–186.) Experiment with different patterns and colors. Here's how you make a knotted bracelet.

You Will Need:

- **Lightweight cord or embroidery thread**

1. Pick four strands of cord or embroidery thread whose length is three times the circumference of your wrist.

2. Tie the cord at the loop tops.

3. Bring the right two cords over the left two cords.

4. Form a loop on the right side.

5. Bring the right cords behind the left cords and then through the loop on the right.

6. Then bring the left cords over the right cords.

7. Form a loop on the left side.

8. Bring the left cords behind the right cords and then through the loop on the left side.

9. Continue to tie knots from right to left.

10. Finish your bracelet with a bead a little larger than your beginning loop and use the bead to fasten the bracelet on your wrist.

Variations: You can insert beads at steps 5 and 8.

Scrimshaw Pin

Try a modern-day variation of scrimshaw, the art of carving a pattern or drawing on ivory or whalebone, to make a pin. Because of environmental concerns, ivory and whalebone are no longer used, but you can create the same results on hard plastic.

You Will Need:

- **A white candle or piece of white wax**
- **A piece of flat white or light-colored plastic**
- **A large-size sewing needle**
- **Black crayon**
- **Soft cloth**
- **Glue**
- **Pin back**

1. Rub the surface of the plastic with the candle or wax to fill in any nicks or rough surfaces. Wipe the surface.

2. With the needle, scratch a design on the plastic.

3. Rub the crayon over the scratches so the crayon wax fills in the marks you have made.

4. Use the cloth to wipe away the crayon. The crayon should remain in the lines of the design. (To see your design develop, do a few scratch marks, use your crayon, then wipe. Repeat these three steps until your design is finished.)

5. Seal your design with varnish or clear nail polish.

6. Glue on a pin back and you're ready to wear your new jewelry.

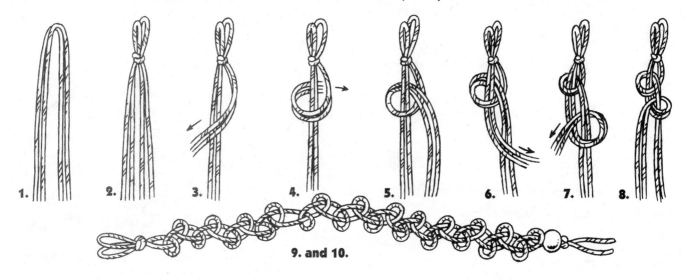

1. 2. 3. 4. 5. 6. 7. 8.

9. and 10.

Catch Board

This board can be used to hang keys, memo pads, eyeglasses, or jewelry.

You Will Need:

- **A flat, wooden board**
- **At least 12 nails (each about 2″ or 5 cm long)**
- **A hammer**
- **Medium-grain sandpaper**
- **A small block of wood (about the size of a bar of soap)**
- **A paintbrush**
- **Pliers**
- **A rag**
- **Heavy cord or string**
- **A saw**
- **Paint or clear varnish**
- **A drill (or 2 ring-topped screws)**

1. Saw the board to measure 12" by 18" (30 cm by 46 cm).

2. Wrap the sandpaper around the small wood block, and smooth the edges and surface of the board.

3. Rub the board with a rag to remove any dust.

4. Paint or varnish the board. You can: paint designs; paste on pictures, drawings, or decorative pieces of paper and then coat with a clear varnish; draw with a permanent ink marker and then coat with a clear varnish.

5. Let your decorated board dry for at least 24 hours.

6. Hammer the nails 1/2" to 1" (1 1/4 cm to 2 1/2 cm) deep in assorted places on the board. The nails can coordinate with your design. Whatever you want to keep on the board will hang from these nails.

7. Grip the nail heads with the pliers and bend each nail upward.

8. You can prepare the board for hanging in two different ways. Use method A if you have a drill for making holes; use method B if you do not.

A. Drill holes in the top corners of the board.

B. You will need two ring-topped screws for this hanging method. These screws will go on the top corners of the board. Start holes for the screws by using an awl or by gently hammering nails into the spots for the screws. Pull the nails out and put the screws into place. Turn them until they fit tightly. If turning becomes difficult, insert a screwdriver through the opening and turn.

9. Thread the cord through the holes (or rings) and then knot the ends so that the cord will not pull through.

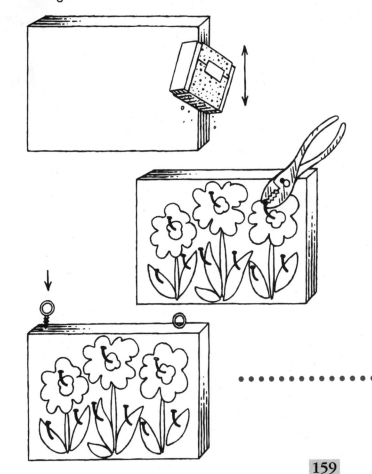

Science is the search for the what, how, and why of things, and the knowledge that comes from that search.

Technology is the application of science. It is using what people have learned about the why and how of the world to create practical things–things that help people live.

For example, a bird can fluff its feathers to create air spaces, which insulate the bird from the cold. So the warm, lightweight jacket you wear may use material that imitates bird feathers, or it can be made out of the real thing!

Have you ever wondered:

▲ How ducks stay warm in cold water?

▲ Why bubbles are round?

▲ How a computer works?

What Can You Live Without?

Try this game with friends. List 15 items made possible by technology, or the application of science. The items should be things that are important to you. Then cut the list down to ten items that everyone agrees she can live without. Then cut it down to five items. Talk about why particular things were chosen.

Technology

Sharpening Your Observational and Investigative Skills

Observation is an important part of doing science. Here are activities to help sharpen your skills in observation.

Science and Technology Hunt

Find examples of science at work for each of the following and ask yourself why and how it works.

- ▲ A chemical reaction
- ▲ A liquid turning to a solid
- ▲ Something conducting heat
- ▲ Something stopping and going
- ▲ An action that causes a reaction
- ▲ A gear or a pulley at work
- ▲ Light traveling

- ▲ Sound traveling
- ▲ Colors mixing
- ▲ Water changing to gas
- ▲ Electricity traveling
- ▲ A magnet attracting
- ▲ Crystals being used

Artist and Scientist

Here are some words used to describe the way an object looks:

- ▲ Shape—circular, square, oval, trapezoidal
- ▲ Size—inches, centimeters, feet, meters
- ▲ Texture—rough, smooth, slick, gritty
- ▲ Directions—right, left, up, down
- ▲ In relation to—at a right angle to, parallel to, horizontal to, vertical to, smaller than, larger than
- ▲ Color—hue, shaded, intense

You Will Need:

- ▲ An assortment of objects that can be held easily (for example, a bird feather, a pine cone, a coffee cup, macaroni, a stamp) and that are not immediately recognized by description
- ▲ A pad of paper and a pencil for each set of partners

1. With a partner, sit back to back. One person is the artist and the other is the scientist.

2. The scientist holds an object that the artist has not seen. She must describe the object to the artist, who draws what is described.

3. When the artist is done, compare the drawing with the actual item.

You can see why it is important to use as many descriptive terms as possible! Change places and repeat the process with a different item.

Pendulums are used to keep time on many different kinds of clocks, but you can use a pendulum to create patterns.

You Will Need:

▲ A 6" or 15 cm square of stiff construction paper

▲ Sand or salt

▲ String

▲ A thumbtack

▲ A large sheet of dark construction paper

▲ Scissors or a pin

▲ Chair or tabletop

▲ Hole puncher

▲ Glue

1. Fold the paper square in half to form a triangle, then again to form a smaller triangle. Open to form a cone. Tape sides to secure the cone.

2. Cut a small opening in the tip of the cone or pierce it with a pin. Punch holes in the longer tips of the paper cone and thread with string. Tie these ends to a longer string and suspend from a tabletop or chair.

3. Place construction paper under the cone. Fill the cone with salt or sand, holding a fingertip on the bottom opening. Swing the pendulum from the center and release it. (The design can be fixed by coating the construction paper ahead of time with a thin coat of white household glue.)

Try getting the pendulum to go straight back and forth and in spirals. What do you notice about the patterns?

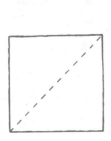
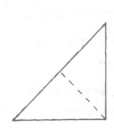

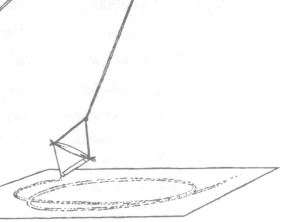

Chemical Appearing Act

You can do an appearing act by using a chemical reaction to make an artistic design become visible. Sometimes, when chemicals react with each other, the result is a color change. Try this and have chemistry bring your work of art out for all to see.

You Will Need:

▲ **White vellum tracing paper (available at art supply stores)**

▲ **A wide paintbrush**

▲ **An artist's thin paintbrush or flat nib pen**

▲ **Starch solution**

▲ **Iodine/alcohol solution**

1. Place tracing paper over a drawing that has heavy enough lines so tracing can be done easily.

2. Dip the thin brush or pen in the starch solution and trace the drawing. If you are using a pen, be careful not to scratch the paper. Starch solution is colorless, so when it is dry, nothing will show on the paper.

3. Tape the corners of the paper to minimize curling. Dip the wide brush into the iodine/alcohol solution and, taking care not to rub, gently stroke over the tracing. Bluish-purplish lines will appear as the iodine chemically reacts with the starch.

Try some other activities using this chemical reaction: send a secret message, make a buried treasure map, put on a magic show for younger children.

Starch Solution: Mix 4 tablespoons (60 ml) of cornstarch in 1 cup (235 ml) of lukewarm water. Cooking water from potatoes or pasta may also be used.

Iodine/Alcohol Solution: Mix 1 tablespoon (15 ml) of tincture of iodine in 1 cup (235 ml) of rubbing alcohol. This solution will have a yellowish-brown color.

Compass Maker

Compasses work because the earth is like a giant magnet. When something is magnetized, it points to magnetic north. You can use that knowledge to make your own compass as the sailors did long ago. (See "Finding Your Way with a Compass," pages 181–182, to learn more about compasses.)

You Will Need:

▲ A strong magnet

▲ A needle (that will stick to the magnet)

▲ A cork big enough to lay the needle on

▲ A thumbtack

▲ A bowl of water

▲ A paper clip

▲ A real compass

▲ A dab of colored nail polish

1. Stroke the needle along the magnet one way until it acts like a magnet and attracts the paper clip.

2. Poke the thumbtack into the bottom of the cork to keep it from tipping over.

3. Lay the cork in the bowl of water so it floats in the middle. Lay the needle so it is flat on the cork.

4. Use a real compass to check which way your needle is pointing. Put a dab of nail polish on the end pointing north. Determine the cardinal points of your compass (North, South, East, West).

Environmental Observer

You don't always have to use the equipment of a scientist to decide whether a place is healthy or not for plants and animals to live (that includes you!). The Stream Health Checklist shown here tells you what to look for, smell, and touch to determine how healthy a stream is. Use the checklist to make an environmental report card for stream exploration, or develop your own list of checkpoints for an area you want to explore.

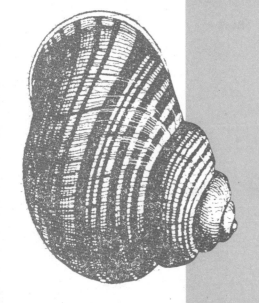

Stream Health Checklist

	Good	Fair	Poor
Variety of stream animals (fish, snails, insects, worms, and other living creatures). The greater the number of types, or species, the healthier the stream.			
Shade from overhanging vegetation.			
Stability (lack of erosion) of stream bank.			
Clearness of water.			
Turbidity of water (amount of stuff suspended in the water). Does water appear cloudy or clear?			
Smell of water.			
Signs of run-off from surrounding land.			
Amount of garbage along stream.			

Use your report card to encourage others to care for the stream in some way.

"Key" Maker

Scientists need ways to sort, or classify, things so they can study them, describe them, and identify them again. A written or illustrated classification of things is called a key. Here's a way to develop your own simple key.

You Will Need:

▲ **An assortment of things, such as different kinds of trees, leaves, shoes, things you write with, or even people**

▲ **Paper and a pencil**

1. Gather all your samples.

2. Think of a way to divide your pile into two groups.

Then write one or two words to describe each group (for example, "leafy" and "needle").

3. Now divide each group into two more groups (for example, "hand-shaped," "oval," "short," "long").

4. Continue dividing and adding descriptions until each group contains only one thing.

5. Regather your things and start over. Create a new key with a new set of descriptions.

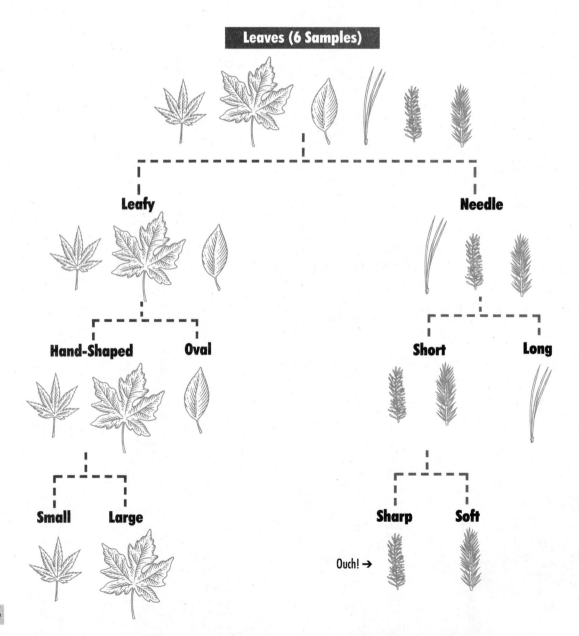

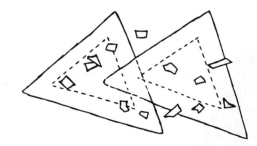

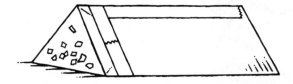

You Will Need:

▲ **A shiny picture postcard**

▲ **Tape**

▲ **Colored cellophane**

▲ **White tissue paper**

▲ **Scissors**

1. Fold the postcard, with shiny side in, lengthwise into three equal sections. (Can you do it without a ruler?)

2. Tape the postcard (now a triangular tube) so the seam doesn't leak light.

3. Cut small pieces of colored cellophane.

4. Cut two pieces of white tissue paper 2" (5 cm) larger than the end of the tube.

5. Place the cut cellophane between the two pieces of tissue paper and tape around one end of the tube. You now have a kaleidoscope that relies on reflected light to create its special effects. Hold it up to the light. What do you see?

Using your kaleidoscope, find different reflections. Have a kaleidoscope party and ask others to bring different kinds of kaleidoscopes.

Science Challenge:

How do you make grass grow quickly using sunlight?

You Will Need:

•A sponge

•Water

•Grass seed

•A glass

•A saucer

Answer: Put some grass seed on a moist sponge, cover with a glass, and leave in the sunlight for several days. The glass acts as a greenhouse, producing heat and water in a contained environment.

Have you ever blown bubbles? Now is the time for some scientific bubble studies!

You Will Need:

To make a bubble solution:

▲ 1 cup (235 ml) of liquid dish soap

▲ 40-50 drops of glycerin (available at a drugstore)

▲ A 1-gallon plastic jug

▲ Enough water to fill up a 1-gallon jug

Mix ingredients in the plastic jug and let sit for 12 hours, if possible.

To study bubbles:

▲ Things to blow bubbles through such as drinking straws, plastic berry baskets, canning rings

▲ Rulers

▲ Smooth tabletops or plastic trays or pans

▲ Towels or rags

What Holds Bubbles Together?

Water molecules on the surface of water tend to stick together. This is called surface tension. When soap is added, it reduces the surface tension of water, allowing the bubbles to form. Bubbles pop when water evaporates out of the bubbles. Adding glycerin helps strengthen the bubbles by preventing the water from evaporating. If you want to touch a bubble without bursting it, wet your hand.

Bubbles are round when floating in the air because of air pressure. The air outside the bubble presses inward while the air trapped inside the bubble presses outward.

The colors you see when you look at a bubble are from light reflecting off the soapy coating on the water molecules. This soapy film is on the water molecules in layers, like paint in various thicknesses.

Make Bubbles and Bubble Domes

1. First, practice blowing bubbles. Dip berry baskets and other tools in the bubble solution. Blow air into the tool or move the tool through the air. Experiment with sizes and shapes.

2. Blow bubble domes (half-spheres) onto a tray or shallow pan by capturing bubble solution in a straw. Hold the straw just at the surface of the pan and blow gently. Carefully remove the straw.

Bubble Domes

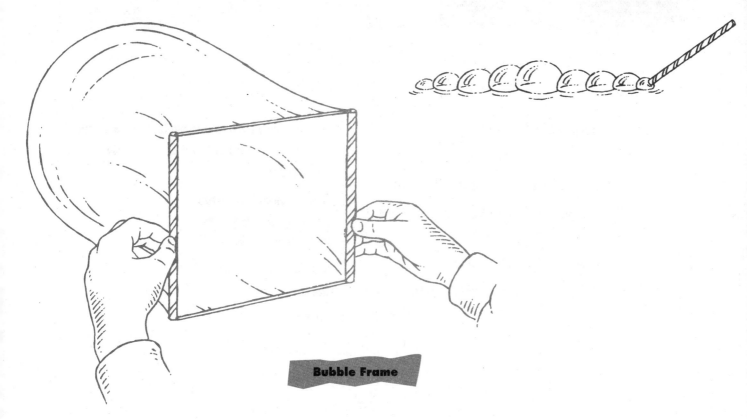

Bubble Frame

Make a Bubble Frame

1. Cut two equal pieces of straw and run about 18" (46 cm) of string through the pieces of straw.

2. Knot the string.

3. Pull the knot into a straw.

4. Form a frame as shown, and lay the frame in the bubble solution (in a pan).

5. Lift it out carefully so you have a soap window across the frame. Make different frame sizes and shapes.

Look for rainbow colors in the frame and move the frame to form different shapes. Can you get another person to put a hand through your frame without bursting it? Make a super bubble by moving the frame slowly through the air. If you want to set your bubble free, pull the two straws together. This takes practice. Avoid popping the bubble in your face and eyes.

Watch your bubbles. Look for size, motion, and color. What happens when they touch?

Making Things Move

Technology has helped people improve the way they move themselves and things from place to place. Observe some simple movement principles in action with the following activities.

Pulleys can help you lift and move things more easily. A pulley is a wheel, and when you add a rope, it becomes a mover or a lifter. Real pulleys have grooves in the wheel to hold the rope.

You Will Need:

▲ 1 thread spool (wooden, if possible)

▲ A wire hanger or heavy-gauge wire

▲ A pole suspended between two chairs, or a hook on a door

▲ A small basket or bucket

▲ 10' (3 meters) of string or cord

1. Bend the wire into a triangle or untwist the hanger to thread the spool as shown. Now you have a pulley.

2. Run the cord over the pulley suspended from the pole or hook.

3. Attach one end of the cord to a basket.

Is it easier to lift the basket with the pulley or without? Experiment with the length of cord needed to lift the load. How much cord do you need to raise the basket a foot off the ground?

Science Challenge

Science Challenge: How do you make a book move across a bare floor using one finger? (Imagine the book is a big stone for a wall you are building.)

You Will Need:

▲ 1 big book

▲ 4 pencils

Answer: Lay the pencils in rows under the book and roll the book forward. Pick up the last pencil and place it in front of the book. This reduces friction between the book and the floor. Try rolling the book with one finger.

Science Challenge: How can you blow up a balloon without blowing into it?

You Will Need:

▲ Large-size plastic soda bottles (empty, with the cap removed)

▲ Balloons

▲ Dish or bowl with very hot water

Answer: Blow up the balloon and then let the air out. This will help stretch the balloon. Put the balloon over the top of the bottle. Now stand the bottle in the bowl of hot water. The heat from the water will warm the air inside the bottle and cause it to expand. What do you think will happen if you leave the open bottle in a refrigerator or a freezer before putting on the balloon and warming? Try it. Does this experiment show you anything about how hot air balloons work?

ACID		ACID RAIN
	0	
	1	Battery acid
	2	Stomach juices
	3	Apple juice, soft drinks
	4	Tomato juice
	5	Black coffee
	6	Normal rain water
	7	Pure water—NEUTRAL
ALKALINE	8	Human blood
	9	Seawater
	10	Milk of magnesia
	11	Household ammonia
	12	Washing soda
	13	Lye
	14	

Simplified pH scale

Scientists group chemicals that have common properties. pH describes how acid or how alkaline (base) a substance is. Acids are sour chemicals. Bases are the opposite. The pH of a chemical is measured by a special scale developed by scientists. The scale runs from 0 to 14, with the middle being 7 (or neutral), with 0 being the most acid, and with 14 being the most alkaline.

Radish pH Tester

How do you test for pH? Set up a testing procedure to determine whether a substance is an acid or a base.

You Will Need:

- Radishes
- Tablespoons
- Water
- Small, clear glasses or plastic cups
- Knife
- Substances to test, such as milk, tomato juice, distilled water, vinegar, lemon juice, tap water, milk of magnesia, baking soda dissolved in water, chalk ground up in water

1. Scrape the skin from one radish into one glass of water. Scrape enough to turn the water a pinkish color. (Use your fingernail or the edge of a dull knife.) The pinkish water is the "tester."

2. Pour small amounts (about 2 tablespoons or 30 ml) of the tester into empty, clean glasses. Use as many glasses as you have substances.

3. Test for acid or base by adding a few drops of the liquid you want to test.

4. Here is what to look for:

Pink color changes to red = an acid

Pink color changes to bluish-green = a base

No color change = neutral

Once you know whether something is an acid or a base, try adding the opposite to see if the color changes again. You can also make a pH tester with red cabbage juice.

Instead of using radish juice to test pH, you can buy a specially treated paper, called litmus paper (narrow range), from a drugstore. Follow the directions on the package to test substances.

Acid and Base in Foods

Some foods contain acids. Lemon juice and vinegar both contain acids. They taste sour. But, many acids and bases are harmful to people. Bases have no strong taste in foods, and often feel slippery or soapy to the touch. Liquid bleach is a base.

Water and soil are tested for their pH. If a swimming pool is too acid, it will burn your eyes. If a pond is too acid, the fish will die. Something acid can be made less so by adding a base. Gardeners, fish biologists, and pool attendants often act as chemists when they test and change the pH of the soil or water by adding an acid or base.

Acid Rain

Some parts of the country and the world have problems with acid rain. This is when rainwater has combined with chemicals in the air from car exhaust or factory smoke to form harmful acidic chemicals.

To see what acid rain will do to buildings, try this experiment, using chalk as your building stone. (Did you test the pH of chalk?)

You Will Need:

- 2 small bowls: 1 filled with water, 1 filled with vinegar or lemon juice
- 2 pieces of new chalk
- A ruler

1. Place the chalk in each of the bowls. What happens?

2. Leave the bowls for 12 hours. Are there still bubbles?

3. Take the chalk pieces out and compare them. What has happened? Why?

Can you find any buildings or stones (such as cemetery gravestones) affected by acid rain in your community?

Computers

Computers are like mechanical brains. People program computers or use already programmed software that tells the computer what to do.

HANDBOOK ACTIVITY

Ask someone to show you how a computer works. Find out the difference between computer hardware and software. Find out about the following computer hardware:

- **Keyboard**
- **Mouse**
- **Printer**
- **Disk drive**
- **Monitor**
- **Desktop, laptop, and notebook computers**

Use several different kinds of computer software. You might visit a computer store and ask for a demonstration.

Think Like a Computer

Write out all the steps for doing something simple, like eating, combing your hair, getting dressed, or fixing your favorite snack. Make a chart that shows the steps. Here's how:

1. Write questions in the pink diamonds.

2. Write information in the orange rectangles.

3. Write instructions in the green rectangles with the rounded corners.

4. Connect these different shapes with lines and arrows.

To get an idea of how this is done, follow "Steps in a Guessing Game" on the next page. Computer programmers call this type of diagram a flowchart.

173

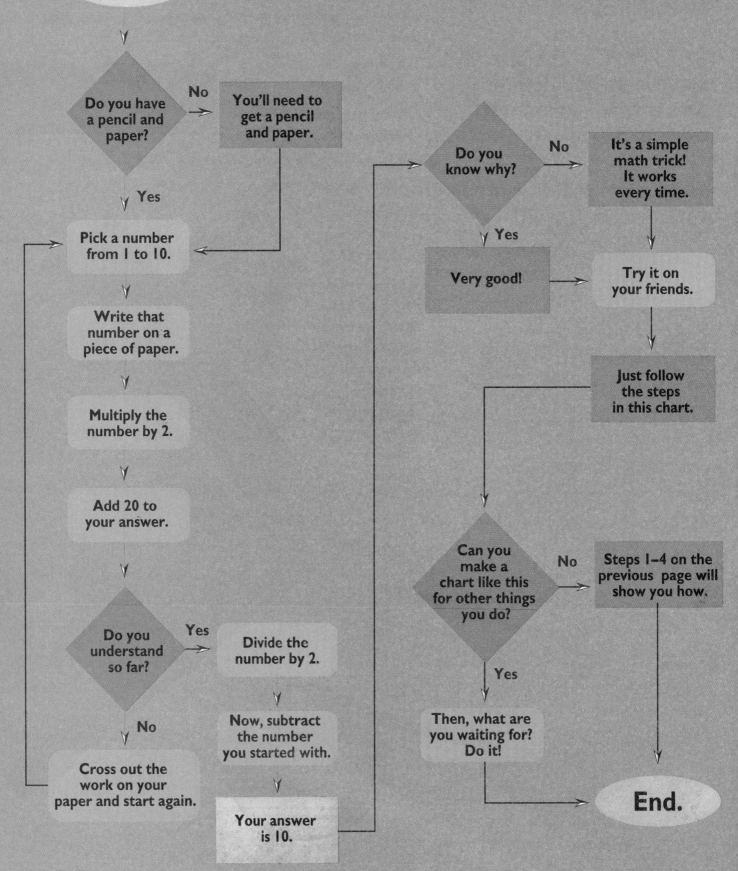

Do you have a pencil and paper?

No → You'll need to get a pencil and paper.

Yes ↓

Pick a number from 1 to 10.

Write that number on a piece of paper.

Multiply the number by 2.

Add 20 to your answer.

Do you understand so far?

Yes → Divide the number by 2.

Now, subtract the number you started with.

Your answer is 10.

No ↓

Cross out the work on your paper and start again.

Do you know why?

No → It's a simple math trick! It works every time.

Yes ↓

Very good! → Try it on your friends.

Just follow the steps in this chart.

Can you make a chart like this for other things you do?

No → Steps 1–4 on the previous page will show you how.

Yes ↓

Then, what are you waiting for? Do it!

End.

174

Computer Talk

Did you know that you could talk to people, shop for clothes, or find information by using a computer? Here's how it works.

You Will Need:

• A computer

• A computer modem, a device that hooks the computer up to the telephone line

• Telecommunications computer software that lets your computer talk to other computers

How it is set up: The modem is connected between the computer and a telephone line. When you dial a computer network service with your modem in place, your computer connects to other computers, called servers. These computer servers have a lot more storage space than your own computer and they collect and store information. (Many computer servers speak to each other through Internet, a global network, or other commercial services. Some don't cost money, but many have a monthly fee for the amount of time used.)

What your options are: Once you are linked to a server, or are "on-line," you have a lot of options, just like going to a shopping mall. Within each option are further selections, just like in each store you visit. Here are some examples of what you might select:

E-Mail: You can send a message by E-mail (electronic mail) to someone in the same room or clear across the country. It takes 10 seconds for a message to go from the United States to Europe. You can link up to "bulletin boards" which contain messages sent by people interested in the same subjects.

Information files: There are many electronic filing cabinets that store information on every subject imaginable. You can search for something on cats or send in your own report on a rare plant you have found.

Services to make life easier: You can order pizza, shop for school clothes, or make airline reservations.

Games: You can hook up with others to play computer games.

What happens if you need help? Most of the computer servers will talk you through questions and problems. Some are more "user-friendly" than others. Many of the computer and software companies have "800" telephone numbers (there is no charge) you can call to get help.

 Note: Although you are cautioned not to speak to strangers in person, different rules seem to be at work on computer networks, where people "talk" to others they have never met. Beware of giving out your phone number, address, and any credit-card numbers on a computer network. Computers and software usually have special programs to prevent others from entering your computer through the network, or to prevent computer viruses from infecting your system.

 Make up a play or game that demonstrates your understanding of computer networks. Investigate how they work and what they cost. If possible, access a computer network at home, school, library, or elswhere and send a message on E-mail.

For more activities involving computers, see the Computer Fun badge in *Girl Scout Badges and Signs*.

Server Computer

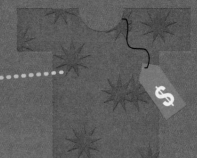
Personal Services

E-Mail

Information Files

Computer Games

Modem

Computer Talk!

Communications Software

Software

Your Computer

Girl Scouts have always used the outdoors for activities. The 1912 Handbook for Girl Scouts *encouraged girls "to meet out, follow open-air pursuits and to camp out in order to learn to appreciate nature to the fullest." Girls learned how to semaphore (use flags to signal the letters of the alphabet), stop runaway horses, shoot an arrow with a bow, and identify plants. They hiked, camped, and grew gardens for feeding themselves.*

Today, open-air pursuits include playing outdoor sports, hiking, camping, biking, gardening, learning about nature, flying a kite, stargazing, snowshoeing, bird-watching, and other activities such as service projects. Add some of your favorite outdoor activities to this list.

Preparing for Outdoor Activities

Every time you prepare for an outdoor activity, remember to plan ahead, learn the skills you need, dress right, keep safe, and practice minimal impact in the outdoors.

Plan Ahead

Deciding where the outdoor activity or camping trip will take place is an important first step in planning outdoor activities. Your troop or group might want to brainstorm ideas to help choose a site and determine what you will do when you get there. (See pages 28–30 for the Travel Action Plan steps.)

Allow time to plan. One meeting is barely enough time to plan a hike; planning an overnight in a place you've never been to would require several meetings. Make telephone calls to find out about places. Get maps and brochures that tell you how far places are. Contact Chambers of Commerce or organizations to find out when places are open and what special programs are offered.

177

By the time you're ready to plan a camping trip, you will have had outdoor experiences close to home. Perhaps you've planned and enjoyed a hike or have had other outdoor experiences. Simple outdoor pursuits should come before camping.

When you're ready to plan a camping trip, the Troop Camper badge in *Girl Scout Badges and Signs* might be a good place to start. Another source of information is an adult from your council who is trained in camping and outdoor activities. Outdoor flag ceremonies, a Girl Scouts' Own, and special evening campfire programs can all be a part of your camping experience.

As you learn about camping, you may want to do more advanced camping, like pitching tents at resident camp, staying at a state park, or planning an overnight backpacking trip. You may want to become skilled at outdoor cooking, orienteering, canoeing, or other outdoor pursuits. Don't forget to explore the possibilities at your Girl Scout council's summer events or resident camp.

Camping "Prep" List

Use this list to plan an overnight camping trip. You might need a separate list for cooking and sleeping gear.

You Will Need:

- **Adults to help you**
- **Parent/guardian permission slips**
- **Arrangements for the site (usually reservations are needed)**
- **Arrangements for transportation**
- **A schedule of activities**
- **Cooking equipment**
- **Menu and food**
- **Sleeping gear**
- **Kaper chart**
- **First-aid kit**
- **Personal items (proper clothing, personal hygiene items, any medications with directions for use, and day-pack items)**
- **Other resources (such as money, maps, compass, flashlight, or games)**

Learning the Skills You Need

Decide which new skills you might need for your outdoor activity. Practice some of these before you set out. For example, learn how to read a map, use a compass, or follow trail markers. Learning how to dress for the outdoors is another skill you should learn.

Dressing for the Outdoors

"Be Prepared" is the best guide for choosing outdoor clothing. Always hope for the best with weather, but prepare for the worst.

Packing Your Day Pack

What do you put in your day pack? What would you carry in your day pack for a hike in the city? What about a hike in the woods? Write your items and see if they match the list that follows.

_____   _____

_____   _____

_____   _____

_____   _____

Basic day-pack contents:

•A water bottle. You need to replace water because you perspire, even on cold days. Use a plastic soda or water bottle.

•A whistle. Use this if you get lost or separated from the group. It saves energy and reduces stress in a scary situation.

•A small mirror for signaling if you get lost.

•Rain gear. This can be a poncho, or a windbreaker and rain pants. Be prepared!

•A quarter for emergency phone calls, along with emergency phone numbers.

•Sunscreen and/or lip protection. Use this to protect from sun and wind.

•A pencil and paper.

•A map or transportation schedule when traveling.

•A portable snack, such as a granola bar, an apple, a piece of hard candy, or "gorp," which can give you a quick surge of energy.

> RECIPE FOR GORP
> 1/2 cup roasted or boiled peanuts
> 1/2 cup sunflower seeds
> 1/2 cup raisins
> 1/2 cup chocolate chips
> 1/2 cup chopped dried fruit
> 1 cup unsugared dry cereal (not flakes)

Learning Camping Skills

The following are important camping skills.

❀ Making a fire

❀ Using a knife safely

❀ Making a bedroll

❀ Tying knots

❀ Doing dishes and disposing of waste

❀ Cooking on a gas stove outdoors

Read the section "Useful Skills for Outdoor Adventures" for instructions on some of these skills.

Keeping Safe

Safety is, of course, very important. So, with the help of your leader, review *Safety-Wise* checkpoints for the activity you are going to do. You also need to take responsibility for bringing permission slips signed by your parent or guardian and notifying your leader of any medical concerns you might have, like an allergy to bee stings. To help stay safe:

❀ Talk to someone who has visited or knows the outdoor place you plan to go. You might want to know whether or not there are bathrooms, clean drinking water, or a place to buy food or supplies, for example. You may have questions about the terrain (is the site hilly?) or animals (are there any to avoid?).

❀ Make sure you are physically fit. If you plan to hike or bicycle, get in shape so you can really enjoy it!

❀ Learn about symptoms and first-aid treatment for emergencies in hot and cold temperatures (see pages 79–80).

❀ Only drink water that you know is from a safe source, like a city or county water supply. (Any water from lakes or streams must be purified before drinking to kill microscopic organisms that will make you sick.)

❀ Carry your own water and drink regularly to avoid getting dehydrated. This is especially important when you are working hard or when it is hot.

Look at the following list. How do these things impact the environment? Discuss what you would do instead if you practiced minimal-impact living skills. You might make a poster to illustrate your discussion.

- **Picking wildflowers**
- **Littering**
- **Dumping soapy water near a lake**
- **Not staying on the trail**
- **Leaving garbage**
- **Using non-recyclable drink containers**
- **Feeding wildlife**
- **Playing a loud radio**
- **Chopping down a tree**
- **Using a too-large campfire**
- **Rearranging nature**

❀ Always have a plan to follow if you should get lost. All girls must know what to do if they become separated from the group.

Practicing Minimal-Impact Skills

An unwritten motto of Girl Scouts has always been to leave a place the same way you found it, or in better condition. That is what minimal-impact living means. Everything you do in the outdoors affects the environment in some way. The air you breathe, the water you swim in, and the soil you walk on are all part of the environment, and together with plants and animals, make up the ecosystem you live in. Minimal-impact skills are actions you take to live with the environment. They can be practiced anywhere in the outdoors: while picnicking in the local park, backpacking in the mountains, or exploring a coral reef underwater.

Taking Care of the Ecosystem

Since you are a part of the ecosystem, think about conserving and using resources wisely. When you conserve, you keep something from being damaged or wasted. For example, you need to use water, but you can conserve it by taking short showers or turning the water off when you are brushing your teeth.

Here are some skills you might use while meeting out, moving out, exploring out, cooking out, sleeping out, and camping out. Be sure your leader or another adult who has been trained by your Girl Scout council in outdoor skills helps you with activities that need special care, such as fire-making, using a camp stove, and handling the jackknife. If you go camping with your troop or group, you may learn other skills, such as pitching a tent, using a bow saw, or hiking with a backpack.

Finding Your Way with a Compass

A compass has a small, magnetized needle, inside the compass housing, that floats in air, water, or oil. The needle (red end) will always turn to point to magnetic north of the earth. When you know where north is, you can find any other direction.

The compass housing (see the compass on the next page) is marked with the 360 degrees of a circle. North, east, south, and west are the four main, or cardinal, points on the compass. If you look at the housing, or divide 360 into four, at what degree reading do you find each of the cardinal points? (Hint: North is at 0° or 360°.)

You need a compass, preferably similar to the one pictured on the next page, that has a transparent base for map reading.

Hold the compass in front of you at waist height, with the direction-of-travel arrow pointing straight ahead. To find north, turn the compass housing until north is on the direction-of-travel arrow. Now, slowly turn your body and feet until the red arrow is pointing in the same direction as the direction-of-travel arrow (the "orienting arrow"). When this happens, you are facing north. Whenever you are facing north, the east is to your right, west is to your left, and south is behind you.

Five Ways You Can Help the Environment

1. Cut down on driving. Carpool with friends, use public transportation, ride your bike, walk.

2. Conserve water. Fix leaky faucets, install a water saver in your shower, use a timer for showers, use the washer or dishwasher only when full.

3. Recycle or reuse items whenever possible. Reuse shopping bags, buy recycled paper, participate in community recycling programs.

4. Help keep air clean. Don't smoke, don't burn trash, do plant trees.

5. Help prevent soil erosion. Stay on trails when hiking or walking.

6. Add your ideas to the list:

_____

_____

_____

For additional ways to help the environment, refer to the Contemporary Issues booklet *Earth Matters: A Challenge for Environmental Action.*

To travel on a north line, look in the distance and follow the direction-of-travel arrow with your eyes. Look for a landmark, like a tree or a rock, in your line of sight. Walk to that object, then line up your red arrow with your direction-of-travel arrow, sight, and continue walking. Try that with other directions!

To travel back the way you came, subtract half of 360° (180°) from your degree reading on your direction-of-travel arrow. Then, set your direction arrow on that reading. Turn your body so that the red arrow lines up with the direction-of-travel arrow, and follow your sighting.

To make your own compass, see page 164.

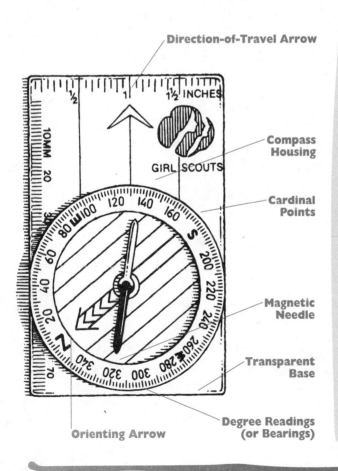

Direction-of-Travel Arrow

Compass Housing

GIRL SCOUTS

Cardinal Points

Magnetic Needle

Transparent Base

Degree Readings (or Bearings)

Orienting Arrow

A Zillion and One Ways to Take a Hike

Choose a theme hike from this list, or create your own, for your next outdoor exploration:

A trail-marker hike. Lay and follow trail markers (see *Outdoor Education in Girl Scouting* for complete directions).

An A-B-C hike. Find a plant or animal starting with each letter of the alphabet.

A throw-away hike. Pick up objects (like fall leaves and dried grasses) as you walk and arrange them on your hands to form a collage.

A spider-eye hike at night. Shine your flashlight beam parallel to the ground in grassy places and look for those red spider eyes.

A picture-story hike. Stop every _____ (yards, blocks, etc.) and frame a picture with your hands. Write a sentence about what you see. Then read all your sentences at the end of the hike.

A career hike. Keep track of how many careers you observe as you walk through an area with people working.

A food-chain hike. Build a food chain as you observe plants and animals that depend upon each other. Try for three to five links, then start over (for example: soil, grass, bug, sparrow, hawk).

A soundless hike. Hike a forest trail without making noise or talking.

A color-palette hike. Look for the primary and secondary colors as you hike.

A water-cycle hike. Look for parts of the water cycle as you hike: precipitation (rain, snow, fog); evaporation (sunlight, dried puddles); run-off (water moving on the ground, storm drains); bodies of water (lake, ocean); flowing water (streams, rivers).

A habitat hike. Look for different homes in the wild.

Math in nature hike. Find the following shapes while hiking: circle, square, hexagon, spiral, diamond, triangle, ellipse (oval).

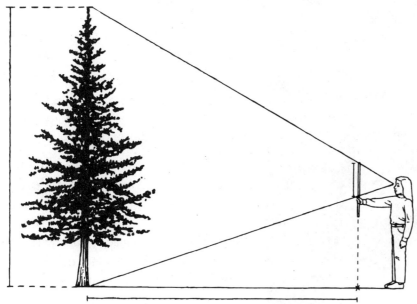

Pacing helps you measure distances as you walk. Once you know how to determine your pace, you can even measure the heights of trees! A pace is defined as two steps.

You Will Need:

• A 50' or 100' (15 or 30 meter) tape measure.

If you don't have a measuring tape, use string marked off in one-foot segments.

To determine your pace:

• Mark off 100' (30 meters) on a flat, straight surface.

• Walk the distance three times, each time writing down how many times your right foot hits the ground. Add up the three distances and divide by three. That number is the length of your pace.

____ + ____ + ____ = _____ **total steps**
÷ 3 = _____ **(the length of your pace)**

To estimate the height of an object using your pace (this works well with trees, flagpoles, or buildings):

• Hold one end of a stick or yardstick upright in your hand, with your arm outstretched in front of your body. The stick above your hand should be the same length as the distance from your outstretched fist to your eye.

• Walk back from the object (make sure you know where you are walking!) until the tip of the stick visually lines up with the top of the object and your thumb covers the bottom of the object.

• Mark the spot on the ground directly below the stick.

• Pace the distance from the mark to the object.

• Multiply the length of your pace times the number of paces you took to find out how high your object is.

Learn to judge distances using knowledge of pace and time. Walk a distance that you know to be one-half mile (1 km) at a comfortable pace. Time how long it takes you. Do this more than once and take an average. Use this knowledge to estimate how far you walk for an unknown distance.

Reading a Map

Maps help you get from one place to another. Maps can help you figure out where you are if you are lost. They can also help estimate distances and tell you if you will be going up or downhill. Reading a map is an important skill to know, whether traveling in your family car, riding on a bus, or hiking in the woods. You can even read a weather map to see an approaching storm.

 Conduct a map symbol hunt. Find as many different kinds of maps as possible, including highway maps, bus maps, park maps, trail maps, topographic (elevation) maps, weather maps, world maps, etc. Look for symbols used on maps, placed in the map legend. Compare the distances represented in each map.

Map Symbols

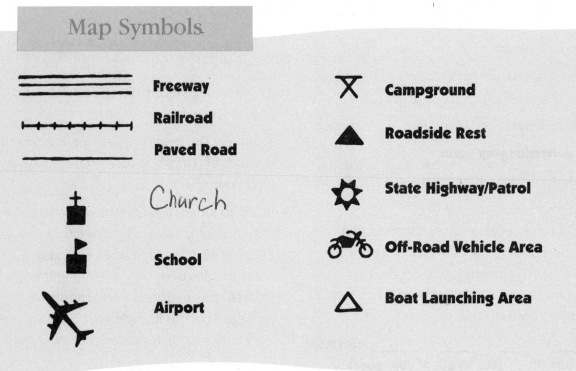

══════ Freeway	✗ Campground
┼┼┼┼┼┼ Railroad	▲ Roadside Rest
─────── Paved Road	✶ State Highway/Patrol
✝ Church	🏍 Off-Road Vehicle Area
⚑ School	△ Boat Launching Area
✈ Airport	

Knots are used for tying packages or doing macramé. You need to know how to tie knots when you put up a tent. Learn basic knots. Then challenge yourself to learn the harder ones!

You Will Need:

• 2 pieces of clothesline or lightweight rope about 12-18" (30-46 cm) long.

• Bright-colored plastic tape

Tape ends of the rope with the plastic tape to keep them from fraying.

Knot	Use	Directions
Overhand	When only a simple knot is needed	
Square	To join two cords of the same thickness	
Half Hitch	To fasten a rope to a ring or tent stake	
Clove Hitch	To fasten one end of a rope to a tree or post	

 Put together a bag full of string tied in knots for your troop or group to practice with or to help younger girls learn how to tie knots.

Knot	Use	Directions
Lark's Head	To loop cord around a ring	
Bowline	To make a loop that won't slip	
Tautline hitch	To make a loop that will slip	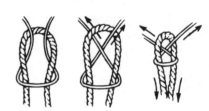
Sheetbend	To tie a thin cord to a thicker cord	
Sheepshank	To shorten a rope	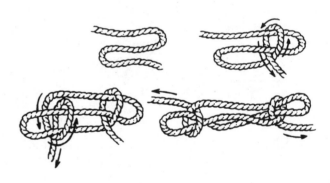

 Decide which knot you would use for the following:

- Shortening a clothesline
- Tying a boat to a dock
- Anchoring a tent to a tent stake
- Tying a rope to a leather dog leash

 Why not try a knot-tying relay game? Divide into teams. Each team gets a piece of cord or string. Each team member selects from a bag a piece of paper with the name of a knot written on it. The first person pulls out the name of a type of knot, ties it, and passes the cord and bag to the second person. The game continues until each team member has tied a knot correctly.

Using a Jackknife

The jackknife is a tool often used when camping. Practice the following safety and care steps, then use your jackknife to slice an apple.

Opening the jackknife: Put your thumbnail in the slot of the blade. Keep your fingers away from the cutting edge. Pull the blade out all the way. Close the jackknife by doing the steps in reverse.

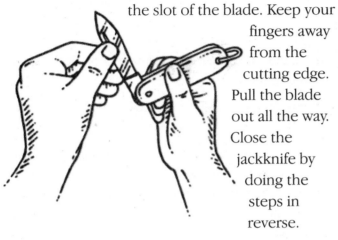

Cleaning the jackknife:
Always keep the jackknife clean and dry. To clean, hold the cloth at the back of the blade, away from the cutting edge. Wipe carefully across the whole blade. Oil the hinge with machine oil. Never clean the blade by rubbing it in dirt or sand. This dulls the blade and makes the knife hard to open and close.

Sharpening the jackknife: A sharp knife is safer and more useful than a dull one. Use a sharpening stone (called a Carborundum or whetstone) to sharpen your knife. Hold the stone in one hand and the open jackknife in the other. Keep fingers below the top of the stone.

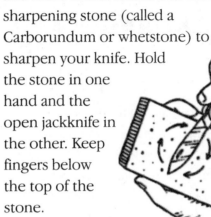

Lay the flat side of the knife blade on the flat surface of the stone. Keep the knife blade almost flat, with the back edge of the blade slightly

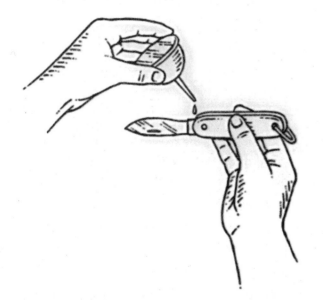

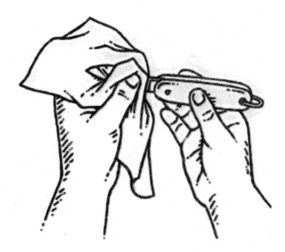

Note: *Before you begin using any sharp tool, be sure there is no one within an arm's length of you (front and sides).*

It's your responsibility to make sure you and others are safe while you use your knife.

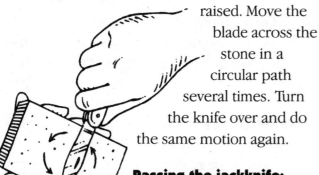

raised. Move the blade across the stone in a circular path several times. Turn the knife over and do the same motion again.

Passing the jackknife:

Always close the jackknife before passing it to another person. If you are passing a knife that doesn't close, grasp the blade along the dull edge of the blade, holding the sharp side away from you, and pass the handle to the other person. This way you have control of the sharp edge. Always say "thank you" when you have received a knife. This signals that you now have control.

Using the jackknife: Hold the handle with your whole hand. Always cut away from you.

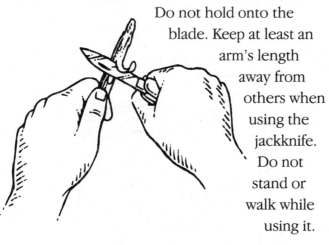

Do not hold onto the blade. Keep at least an arm's length away from others when using the jackknife. Do not stand or walk while using it.

A two-burner gas stove is a great way to cook when camping. It is fast and saves firewood. Review "Portable Cook Stoves" in *Safety-Wise* before using your camp stove.

Before you camp:

•Read the directions for operating your particular stove before you travel.

•Know what kind of fuel your stove needs. Plan to take extra fuel.

•Gather all the equipment you will need for camp-stove cooking: pots, potholders or mitts, wooden matches, safety equipment (such as a trowel and loose earth or sand, baking soda, or a portable fire extinguisher), and a first-aid kit. Take a funnel if you are using gas fuel.

When Using Your Stove:

•Always have an adult present.

•Tie back your hair and do not wear loose clothing.

•Find a safe, level spot outdoors for your stove.

•Clear any debris away from around the stove, and do not use rocks to prop it up.

•Don't place the stove in a windy area. If the stove has a windscreen, put it in place to break the wind.

•Never use the stove in a tent or indoors. This is because it uses the oxygen you breathe and the fuel is dangerous, especially if spilled indoors. Stoves also can give off carbon monoxide, a gas that is harmful to people.

•Read the operating instructions again and light the stove according to the directions. Hold the match so the flame burns upwards.

•Adjust the flame for cooking. Blue flame is the hottest. You may want to soap the outside bottoms of your pans before placing them over the flame so pot scrubbing is easier.

•Do not reach over the stove. When stirring, hold onto the pan with a mitt. On a small, single-burner stove, take the pot off the stove before stirring and then return it.

•Do not leave the stove unattended. If you run out of fuel, turn off the stove and let the stove cool. Refuel away from the stove and any heat source or flame. If fuel is spilled, let it evaporate and do not strike matches nearby. Never remove a fuel container from a stove without turning off the stove first.

•When you are finished cooking, let the stove cool before cleaning. Make sure that gas valves are all tightly turned off before packing.

Checklist for Outdoor Cooking

Whether you are cooking in the backyard or backpacking with a portable stove, you will need:
- A cool, dry place to store food
- A safe place to build your fire or operate your stove
- A place to wash your hands
- A place to fix your food
- A place to eat
- A method for cleaning up
- A place to put garbage and items to be recycled

One-Pot Meal

Try making this stew over a fire or a stove. You need one large pot. Serves four to six.

Vegetarian Chili

1 cup uncooked brown or white rice

1 6-oz. jar tomato paste

2 cubes low-salt chicken or vegetable bouillon

2 12-oz. cans red kidney beans

1 medium onion (chopped)

3 stalks of celery (chopped)

1 medium green or red pepper (seeded and chopped)

1 tablespoon oil

3 carrots (peeled or scrubbed and chopped)

1 tablespoon chili powder

4 cups water

Sauté (fry) the onion and green pepper in the oil until soft. Add celery and carrots and sauté for 2-3 minutes. Add beans with liquid, chili powder, 4 cups of water, tomato paste, and bouillon cubes. Simmer (Heat on a low flame). Add rice. Cook until rice is done—20 minutes for white rice and 50 minutes for brown rice.

Making a Fire

*G*irl Scouts learn how to make fires because it is a skill you can use when appropriate. In the United States, some cities and parks have banned fires because not enough wood is available, or there is a fire or pollution danger. Think about other ways to cook, or plan meals that don't require cooking!

Safety Tips for Making a Fire

Fire-making is a basic survival skill that provides heat for warmth and fuel for cooking. You may build a fire at camp with your troop or group or with your family at a campground. Always check fire-making rules of the area, and follow these safety tips:

• Keep a bucket of water and shovel (for stirring wet coals or placing dirt on the fire to smother it) on hand before building your fire.

• If you are building a fire in a fireplace, make sure the draft in the chimney is open and a screen is placed across the fireplace to prevent sparks from jumping out onto clothing or rugs. If building a fire indoors, observe proper safety rules.

• Tie back your hair and wear long pants.

• Do not start a fire during air-pollution alerts, high winds, or very dry conditions.

(For more about fire-making, see "Cooking Fires" in *Safety-Wise*.)

Before You Make a Fire

A fire needs fuel and air to burn. When making a fire you need three sizes of wood for a fire to last:

Tinder is small material that burns as soon as it is lit with a match. Tinder could be dry wood, dry leaves, or wood shavings.

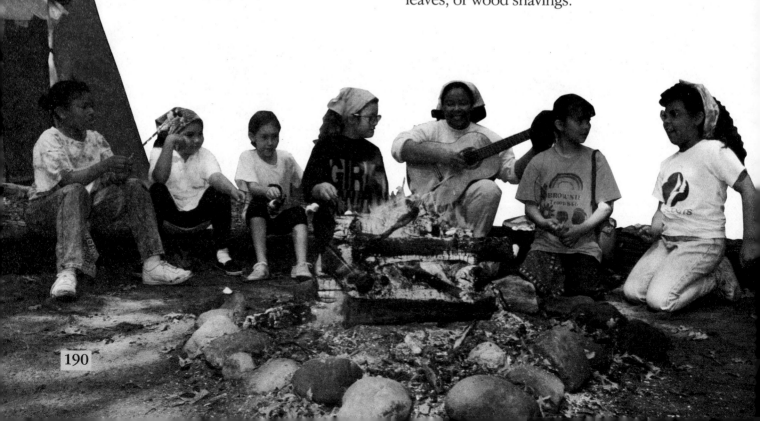

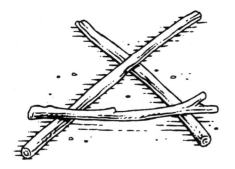

Kindling is larger in diameter than tinder, thin enough to catch fire before the tinder burns out, and large enough to catch the fuel. Kindling should be dry enough to snap.

Fuel is larger wood that keeps a fire going. Fuel should be dry, seasoned wood found lying on the ground or in a woodpile.

When preparing to make a fire, use a fireplace or fire ring. If you need to prepare a fire ring, clear the area down to the soil, and avoid roots, dry materials, and overhanging branches. Have enough tinder, kindling, and fuel on hand so you do not have to leave your fire.

Building a Fire

1. Make a small triangle with three pieces of kindling, leaving an air space under the top bar of the triangle.

2. Lay a handful of tinder against the apex (top) of the triangle, leaving some air space. Lean tinder toward the center, upright. (You can use a combination of tinder and fire-starter at this point.)

3. Strike a wooden match close to the tinder and away from your body. Hold the match under the tinder at ground level so the flame burns upwards.

4. As the tinder catches, add additional tinder carefully, then begin placing kindling so it leans against the triangle above the flaming tinder. Continue adding kindling, building a cone shape.

5. Add fuel (large pieces of wood) to the fire so the kindling can catch it. Leave air spaces, and use only the amount of fuel you need.

Make the fire only as large as you need it. Conserve fuel and avoid smoke pollution.

If you need a concentrated heat source (for boiling water, for example), continue making the cone shape and cook on the flame. You might also use a grate. As the fire burns down, it forms coals. This is the best heat to cook on.

When You Are Finished with a Fire:

1. Let the fire die down until only ashes are left.

2. With a long stick or shovel, stir the ashes, sprinkle them with water, then stir again. Continue until there is no gray ash and the fire bed is cool. Pouring water on a fire can cause steam and rock explosions.

3. Remove any signs that you were there, returning the site to the way you found it. If you've used a fireplace, leave it clean by removing the ashes.

Learn about other ways to cook, such as solar ovens, charcoal fires, or a camp stove.

Some Outdoor Cooking Tips

• One-pot meals are easiest to fix and clean up.

• Boiling water can be used to make a lot of things: gelatin, hot cocoa, soup, pasta, vegetables, instant meals.

• Dry foods, such as jerky, dried fruits, and rice keep without refrigeration.

• Meat and dairy products spoil the most quickly and need to be kept in a refrigerated place.

• Use plastic bags and reusable containers to carry food. Buy food in bulk and repackage for travel.

• Soap the outside of the pot when cooking on a fire. It's much easier to clean.

For more information on outdoor cooking, see *Outdoor Education in Girl Scouting*.

From sports to science to outdoor fun, you have a range of activities to try as a Junior Girl Scout. Sample some of the activities in this chapter and discover a lot about your interests, skills, and talents.

BRIDGING & RECOGNITIONS

CHAPTER 8

In this chapter, you will find information about earning Junior Girl Scout recognitions and bridging to Cadette Girl Scouts. All handbook badges can be found in this chapter and are listed under the badge name. You can also read about the bridging steps, requirements for earning the Sign of the World, and steps for earning the Junior Girl Scout Leadership pin.

Recognitions are badges, signs, and pins you earn as a Junior Girl Scout. They are symbols of your interests and accomplishments. Your *Junior Girl Scout Handbook* and the book *Girl Scout Badges and Signs* have activities to do to earn badges.

Junior Girl Scout Badges

You can find most Junior Girl Scout badges in *Girl Scout Badges and Signs*. This handbook has an additional 13 badges. *Girl Scout Badges and Signs* contains badges with green background colors and tan background colors. The green-backed badges are easier to do and take less time to finish. The badges with tan backgrounds take more planning and more time to complete. The beginning section of *Girl Scout Badges and Signs* has more information on these badges. Your *Junior Girl Scout Handbook* has badges with a white background and a dark blue border. Many badge activities are  included in Chapters One to Seven of this handbook. But *all* handbook badges are included in this chapter. Look for the badge symbol. When you find one, you know that this activity is a badge requirement.

Signs and Other Recognitions

Besides badges, Junior Girl Scouts can earn signs such as the Sign of the World, Rainbow, Satellite, and Sun. Other recognitions you can earn as a Junior Girl Scout are: the Junior Girl Scout Leadership pin, the Junior Aide patch, the Bridge to Cadette Girl Scouts patch, religious recognitions, and patches you may get if you do activities from the Contemporary Issues booklets or go on special events sponsored by your Girl Scout council. (For more about insignia and recognitions, see Chapter One.)

The activities for the Sign of the World, which are included in this handbook, will help you learn more about yourself and your community. The requirements include badge activities. A badge activity can only be counted once in completing any of the signs. Signs should take you longer to earn than badges.

The Junior Aide Patch

You earn the Junior Aide patch when you work with Brownie Girl Scouts. The requirements for earning the Junior Aide patch are in *Girl Scout Badges and Signs*.

Bridging to Cadette Girl Scouts

Moving from one Girl Scout level to another is called bridging. You can begin to bridge to Cadette Girl Scouts in your last year as a Junior Girl Scout. As a Cadette Girl Scout, you can continue to enjoy camping, trips, and

many activities you enjoyed as a Junior Girl Scout, but Cadette Girl Scouts have more freedom, take on more responsibility, and enjoy new opportunities. As a Cadette Girl Scout, you could work on Fashion/Fitness/ Makeup, Understanding Yourself and Others, Space Exploration, or Outdoor Survival interest project activities. You could go on national and international wider opportunities or learn to be a Cadette Girl Scout program aide. Cadette Girl Scouts have dug for dinosaur bones, climbed mountains, worked with children with special needs, helped build houses in Mexico, sailed on tall ships, and visited Pax Lodge in England and Sangam in India.

Cadette Girl Scouts have their own set of special recognitions, including the Cadette Girl Scout Leadership Award, the Cadette Girl Scout Challenge, and the Girl Scout Silver Award. There's room as a Cadette Girl Scout to explore your special interests and use your talents to create a Girl Scout experience that's right for you. When you are ready to take the following bridging steps, you can begin your path to Cadette Girl Scout adventures and earn your Bridge to Cadette Girl Scouts patch.

Step 1: Find out about Cadette Girl Scouting. Look through the *Cadette Girl Scout Handbook* and *Interest Projects for Cadette and Senior Girl Scouts*. Find three activities you would like to do.

Step 2: Do a Cadette Girl Scout activity. Do one of the three activities you chose in Step One.

Step 3: Do something with a Cadette Girl Scout. Visit a Cadette Girl Scout troop or group meeting or help with an activity that a Cadette Girl Scout has planned.

Step 4: Work on a service project with a Cadette Girl Scout. Find out about a service project a Cadette Girl Scout or a group or troop is doing and help out.

Step 5: Be a leader. Do something that builds leadership skills. You could do activity Number One in the Leadership interest project in *Interest Projects for Cadette and Senior Girl Scouts* or assist a leader with a troop or group of younger girls.

Step 6: Share what you learn about Cadette Girl Scouts with others. Talk to other Junior Girl Scouts or visit a Brownie or Daisy Girl Scout troop or group and teach a game or song you learned with Cadette Girl Scouts. Or, make a presentation of the special things about Cadette Girl Scouting.

Step 7: Help plan your bridging ceremony. Plan ways to make your ceremony special. Create or discover some special songs, poems, sayings, or decorations.

Step 8: Find out about opportunities and participate in a summer Girl Scout activity. What opportunities can you create?

Arts and Media

Complete four activities.

Please use extra care when doing art activities.

1. Do one of the music activities on page 151. Share what you learned with your troop or group.

2. Use the ideas on page 152 to create a drawing or painting.

OR Find out what a mural is. With your troop or group, develop an idea and work on a mural.

3. Do the printmaking activity on page 155.

4. Do the decoupage activity on page 153.

5. Read about sculpture on page 156. Make a sculpture of your choice.

OR Try making something using embroidery (see page 157), or find out about another kind of fabric art that interests you. Then, make something to show your troop or group.

6. Read about jewelry-making on pages 157–158 and try one of the activities.

7. Make a catch board (see page 159) following the woodwork instructions. (If you don't want to make a catch board choose another woodworking activity not included here.)

8. Create your own project combining art and music.

Careers

Complete five activities.

1. Think of women you admire. What characteristics do they have that you would like to have? Fill in "My Characteristics" chart on page 111.

2. Find out about community and school drug-prevention projects. Invite someone who works in one of these projects to come and speak to your troop or group.

3. Look at the list of health careers on page 96 and find out more about these jobs. Discover what education or training is required and what the average salaries are.

4. You can choose a career that involves personal care. A hairstylist cuts and styles hair. A dermatologist is a doctor who diagnoses and treats skin problems. Investigate other careers. Invite people who have careers in personal care to visit your Girl Scout troop or group.

5. Fashion designers can become very famous, but there are lots of other jobs in the fashion industry. Find out about careers in the fashion and cosmetics industries; for example, find out about clothing buyers, fashion consultants, personal shoppers, cosmetologists, hairstylists, textile designers, and salespersons. How can you find out about these careers? Maybe you can interview people who have these jobs or career-shadow them for a day.

6. Invite someone who works in the financial industry such as an accountant, bank officer, bank examiner, or personal finance manager to visit your troop or group and explain what she does.

7. Choose five activities from Chapter Seven and brainstorm a list of careers that could match those interests.

8. Look at the list of jobs on page 113. Why not look in the classified advertisements of a newspaper or phone the professional associations or some businesses and find out how much a person makes who has one of these jobs? Compare these salaries with some of the more traditional "female" jobs.

9. Find out about a career you might like to have. Find out about education, special training, and salary (beginning and after ten years). What clothes, tools, or equipment are used in this career? To what other careers does this career lead? If you and the other girls in your troop or group find out about different careers, what are some ways you could share or use this information?

Consumer Power

Complete four activities.

1. Get copies of two or more newspapers printed on the same day, choose one story that is printed in both and compare. Where does the story appear? the front page? later in the newspaper? in a different section?

How long is the story? Is the information the same? What is the tone—the overall impression—of the story? positive, negative, neutral, anxious, upbeat?

2. Watch two or three news shows shown at the same time. Flip back and forth between the shows. Keep a log of what stories are reported, how much time is given to the story, who reports the story (the main newscaster or a reporter), and what differs in the report. Compare your log with other girls in your Girl Scout troop or group.

3. Do the television-viewing guidelines activity on page 119.

4. Do the smart music-video viewing guide activity on page 120.

5. Close your eyes for a moment. What advertisement pops into your head? Why do you remember it? How does this advertisement try to persuade you? In your troop or group, gather in small groups or in pairs and pick an advertisement or commercial to analyze (study carefully). Think of three different ways the advertisement is persuasive. Are there attractive people in the advertisement? Does the advertisement promise something new? What are some other messages the advertisement is sending? Pick one person in your group or pair

to explain to the others what you discovered.

6. Do the food labels activity on page 96.

Discovering Technology

Complete six activities, including the two starred.

 Please use extra care when demonstrating some of the activities in number 6.

*1. Discover how often you rely on technology. Keep a log for a week listing how and when you use technology. Then do the "What Can You Live Without?" activity on page 160 with friends.

2. Discover "Pulley Power." Send a message or lift an object using pulleys. See page 170 for details.

3. Discover how technology is shaping the future. Find out about at least two of the following: voice recognition, virtual reality, lasers, tele-communications, robotics. If possible, use or view one of these technologies.

197

4. Discover how technology has changed the way things are done. Pick at least three careers and find out how technology is used in those professions. Has technology changed those jobs, or the way the jobs are performed? Share your findings with your troop or group by role-playing, participating in a panel discussion, or hosting a discussion by people in different professions.

*5. Discover computer networks. Make up a play or game that demonstrates your understanding of computer networks. Or, investigate how they work and what they cost. Or, access a computer network at home, school, library, or elsewhere and send a message on E-mail.

6. Discover a leisure-time activity that uses technology and share the activity or knowledge of the activity with your troop or group. For example, display photos or a videotape you have taken, sing kareoke, direct a remote-control boat or car, sew something on a sewing machine, use some exercise equipment with the help of an adult, or display greeting cards or a poster you have made from a computer graphics program.

7. Do the Science Challenge "How Do You Make a Book Move Across a Bare Floor Using One Finger?" on page 171.

Girls Are Great

Complete five activities.

1. Prepare a short skit using not only words but also pictures, symbols, and body language to deliver one of the following messages:

- What's special about being a girl?
- What's exciting about growing up?
- Your definition of beauty.

Perform your skit for other members of your troop or group and Daisy and Brownie Girl Scouts.

2. Interview women of different ages and backgrounds to find out what it was like when they were growing up. Talk to your grandmother, aunt, neighbor, older sister, teacher, mother, or Girl Scout leader. What challenges did they face when they were your age? What were their hopes and dreams? Collect their responses in a journal or on a tape recorder. What similar concerns do you have about growing up? What different concerns?

3. Make a list of some things girls seem to be expected to do. For example, your list might include play with dolls, cook meals, or babysit. Make a second list of things that boys seem to be expected to do such as play with trucks, cut the grass, and play basketball. Share your list with others and discuss how you feel about these things.

4. The definition of beauty has changed over the years. Visit your local library to find books or magazines that were published about 10 years ago, 20 years ago, 30 years ago, and so on. Page through the materials and lay some of the pictures you find next to pictures in current books and magazines. Make a list of the differences you find. Share your list with others.

5. Select one of your interests, talents, or hobbies and create a collage or poster that shows the contributions women have made in this area. Be sure to include women from different time periods and women who made important contributions but are not necessarily famous.

6. Complete the following statement: "I love being a girl because..." Ask some of your friends to do the same and then compare and discuss your lists. Were there any statements that caused disagreement?

7. Some mothers work outside the home and others do not. Talk to at least two women in each group to find out how they manage responsibilities. Think about some things you juggle in your own life like school, family, and friends. Did you learn anything from talking to the group of mothers that will help you manage your own responsibilities?

Healthy Living

Complete five activities.

Please use extra care when doing activities in numbers 1 and 10.

1. Choose three things from the "Maintaining Your Home" list on page 104. In your Girl Scout group or troop or with an adult, demonstrate that you know how to do them.

2. In your Girl Scout troop or group, discuss ways you could help each other manage time. Talk about times when you felt you had too little time to do the things you wanted to do. What could you have done differently?

3. Think of some activities that you can do alone or with friends rather than just "hang out." Look at Chapter Seven, which has lots of different activities, and choose three that look interesting. Try them, and introduce them to your friends.

4. Practice making emergency telephone calls in your troop or group or with an adult. Learn how to give the most important information quickly and how to follow the directions given to you. Look at page 81 for some practice situations. Try making up your own.

5. In your troop or group, discuss the stressful things that can happen to kids and teens. Discuss how to deal with stressful situations.

6. Look at some cigarette and alcohol advertisements. In your troop or group, discuss what messages are being sent and how you can make these ads more realistic.

7. In your troop or group, brainstorm some safety situations that fit into the categories of weather, water, personal safety, fire, and emergency preparedness. Role-play safe ways to act.

8. Create a game about safety using the safety information in Chapter Three. You could make a card game, board game, or a wide game (a game in which you move from station to station acting out or doing different activities).

9. Pick a sport. You could look at the sports on pages 148–150. Create a safety checklist, poster, or booklet for that sport.

10. Prepare a meal that uses foods from each of the categories in the food pyramid. Read the tips on page 95.

Leadership

Complete five activities, including the three that are starred.

1. List some leaders. Do the activity on page 133 and discuss what you find out with another person.

2. Interview someone you consider a leader in your community. Before you meet with her, make a list of questions to ask. Include a question about what she learned from her mistakes. Present what you learned from the interview to your troop or group.

*3. Take on a leadership role for three months in your troop, school, or community. Be a leader for a sports team, an art project, a music group, or a computer network. Or, organize a neighborhood service club. Keep a journal of your time spent as a leader.

4. Learn about leadership styles by deciding which style matches each situation in the badge activity on the bottom right of page 134.

5. Discuss ways to avoid stereotypes and sexism when taking on a leadership role. Use the activity in the first column on page 134 as a guide.

6. Read the section on Sidshean O'Brien on page 137 and do the "It's Up to You" activity (see page 137).

*7. Use the chart on page 140 to examine problems in your community. Customize the chart for your school, neighborhood, or community by listing issues and actions that you might take.

*8. Read "Creating a Leadership Action Project" starting on page 141. Plan and carry out a leadership-in-action project to benefit your community.

Looking Your Best

Complete five activities.

 Please use extra care when doing activities in numbers 1, 4, 5, 6, 7, and 8.

1. Mend a piece of your own clothing or ask permission to mend a member of your family's clothing. See pages 101–102 for sewing tips.

2. Put on a fashion show with a theme. You might want to dress for different themes: Fashions for the Outdoors, Fashions for the Future, Fashions for Parties. What other themes can you create?

3. Have a hairstyle party. Try different hairstyles on each other. Look at the ideas on pages 88–89 or look through magazines, talk with older girls or adults, or dream up new hair creations! Remember not to share brushes, combs, and other hair appliances. If you can, take instant pictures or shoot a video of your new styles!

4. Do an aerobic activity at least three times a week, for at least 20 or 30 minutes, with a friend.

Plan on doing different types of activities, so you won't be bored. Walking is a very good exercise. You can play a favorite sport, too, as long as you are moving for at least 20 minutes. Some sports are more aerobic than others. Find out which are the most aerobic.

5. With the help of a trained adult, organize an exercise class for other girls your age. Demonstrate and teach activities that can be used to warm up, work out, and cool down.

6. Look through the sports and outdoor activities in Chapter Seven. Choose two and do them by yourself, with a friend, or with a group.

7. Plan a group health feast. Each person can prepare and bring one healthy food to share. Enjoy!

8. Create a troop or group recipe for a delicious, nutritious snack. Prepare your snack for meetings or trips. Or, create colorful wrappers or packages and sell your snack as a troop money-earning project.

9. Create a "Looking Your Best" booklet, poster, video, or collage that includes the most important tips girls your age need to look their best. Look through Chapter Two for some additional ideas on images of beauty.

10. Investigate what alcohol, drugs, and smoking do to your lungs, skin, and other parts of your body. Share what you learn with others.

Complete six of the following activities, including the one that is starred.

Please use extra care when doing activity numbers 3 and 4.

1. Discover surface tension by becoming a bubbleolgist. Do the activities on pages 168–169.

2. Discover how chemical changes can become art or secret writing. Do the chemical appearing act activity on page 163.

3. Discover more about pH by working with an adult to test water in a lake, river, or pool, or by testing soil pH. See page 172.

4. Discover some things about light and reflection by making the kaleidoscope on page 167.

5. Discover how the brain can be challenged or deceived by learning about optical illusions. Look in books and magazines for puzzles, optical illusions, and after-image art. Try creating your own optical illusions or do the "Hidden Picture" activity on page 154. Explain to your troop or group what you've learned about optical illusions.

6. Do the "Mathematical Moiré" activity on page 155.

7. Discover what's happening in science around you. Using a newspaper, telephone book, or magazine, go on a search for people, places, and things that are science related. As you make your list, you may want to create some categories. (Some examples might be: people—doctor, place—laboratory, things—microscope.) Share your list with others.

8. Share what you know about science discoveries with younger girls. You might use some of the science challenges in this book.

*9. Discover more about science by visiting a hands-on science museum in your area or by participating in a science-activity fair sponsored by your school, Girl Scout council, or service unit. What activities did you enjoy the most?

Complete five activities.

1. Carry out a body-language study. See page 73 for more information.

2. Do the public service program activity on page 45.

3. To explore differences in values, try this activity with friends or family. Think about each statement and decide if you agree, disagree, or are not sure. Explain your feelings and listen carefully to what others say.

- Women in the military should have combat duty.

- Everyone should have the right to carry a gun.

- Watching violence on television encourages a person to act violently.

- Money brings happiness.

4. Pretend you are meeting someone for the first time. Think about who that person might be. Tell how you would introduce yourself to her. Talk about what you would say and how you would keep the friendship going. (See page 61.)

5. Read the situations on pages 73–74 and decide on the best way to respond. Make up your own situations or share a time when you had to choose how to respond.

6. Keeping a journal is a great way to learn about yourself, your values, and your feelings. For the next four weeks, write about what happens to you: a problem you had, a good time you had with a friend, something that upset or disappointed you. Then, reread your journal entries. What have you learned about yourself?

7. Think about a problem you experienced recently with a family member. Maybe you fought with your brother over which television show to watch or argued with your mother over cleaning your room. Review the conflict-resolution steps on page 57 and creative solutions on page 72. Use one of these tools to help work out a family problem.

Wider Opportunities

Complete five activities.

1. Create a brochure listing special places to visit in your community. Visit three or more different tourist attractions and historical sites with friends. Take notes and photos that you can use for your brochure.

2. Organize a travel conference. Each girl picks a state, city, or community she would like to visit and finds out as much as she can through books, magazines, television documentaries, travel agents, people from the area, and people who have traveled to the area. Share this information at the conference.

3. Invite a Cadette or Senior Girl Scout or someone from your Girl Scout council to talk to you and your friends about a wider opportunity. Find out which events and workshops you can attend as a Junior Girl Scout.

4. Learn about wider opportunities offered by councils to Cadette and Senior Girl Scouts across the country. Ask your Girl Scout leader to bring her copy of *Wider Ops* to a troop meeting. Look through it and decide on three wider opportunities you would like to participate in. Make a list of the requirements, cost, location, and equipment you would need.

5. Find out what information is recorded in a passport. Create your own make-believe passport.

6. Page through *Wider Ops* and select an event that appeals to you. Then, figure out how to travel there by car. Collect road maps and chart out the best route. Estimate the number of miles you will travel.

7. Design a wider opportunity for a group of younger Girl Scouts. Work with other Junior Girl Scouts and Girl Scout leaders to investigate the kinds of wider opportunities younger girls would like and would be able to do. Then plan, research, and carry out an appropriate wider opportunity for a sister Daisy or Brownie Girl Scout troop. Make sure you involve Girl Scout leaders in the activity and that you have all the permissions you need.

Complete five activities.

1. Create your own community forum on prejudice or another issue affecting your community.

2. Read about cliques on pages 65–66 and do the diary page activity on page 66.

3. Learn not to stereotype. Do the activity on page 126.

4. Survey your meeting place to see how accessible it is to all people. Then, choose a public building in your community and do a survey. Present your findings to your local government.

5. Interview senior citizens to explore the knowledge and history of senior citizens in your family and neighborhood. Create a list of questions about: the history of your community, the changing roles of women, the differences in children's lives from years past to today, or the impact of historical events on community members. Tape-record, write notes, or make a video of your interview. Make sure to give a copy to the person you interviewed. Share this information with others.

6. Page through books and magazines or scan television programs to find stereotypes. (See pages 126–127 for examples.) Choose an example and show how you would break the stereotype.

7. Find out what services are available for people with disabilities or people in need in your community. Invite someone who works at one of these agencies or organizations to speak to your troop or group.

8. Try to discover all you can about contributions of groups different from your own to your community, county, or state. What did you discover?

Complete five activities.

 Please use extra care when doing activity numbers 6, 7, and 8.

1. Visit an outdoor store or look through outdoor catalogs. Find out which synthetic and natural materials are best for different kinds of weather. Investigate the kinds of equipment used in camping and traveling. Discuss if any of the items can be made or found in less expensive forms.

2. Find out about minimal impact on page 180. Discuss the list on that page with your family and friends before going on an outing.

3. Review the list under "Five Ways You Can Help the Environment" on page 181. Add to the list and then commit to doing at least two items. Express your commitment to help the environment by creating a poster or advertisement, for example, for your troop or group meeting.

4. Learn about classification keys on page 166. Use a simple plant key to identify trees at camp or in your community.

5. Be an artist and scientist in the outdoors. Do the "Artist and Scientist" activity on page 161.

6. Learn to use the camp stove and cook a one-pot meal. (See pages 188–189.)

7. Participate in an outdoor activity that can be enjoyed for a lifetime. Learn to ski, swim, golf, photograph nature, backpack, sketch outdoors, bird-watch, or do something else that people of all ages can do.

8. Take a hike! Pick one of the hikes listed on page 182 and plan to go on a hike with your Girl Scout troop or group or family members.

Sign of the World

By completing the activities in this sign, you will get to know yourself better, learn more about working with others, and gain skills in taking care of yourself and your environment.

1. Complete two badges from this handbook and one badge from the World of People in *Girl Scout Badges and Signs.*

2. Complete five activities from Chapter Two of this handbook.

3. Complete three activities from Chapter Five of this handbook.

4. Complete four activities from Chapter Three or Four of this handbook.

5. Read about leadership in Chapter Six. Plan and carry out a service project using the action plan outline on pages 142–144.

Junior Girl Scout Leadership Pin

The Junior Girl Scout Leadership pin requires you to participate in experiences that build leadership skills. As you progress through the steps, you will uncover the leader inside of you. The steps should be done in order.

STEP ONE

Read Chapter Six, Leadership in Action, in this book. Look at the Leadership Checklist on page 132 and circle the leadership qualities you feel you already have. Put a box around three qualities you need to develop. Talk to your Girl Scout leader, a parent or guardian, or other adult about ways you can develop these qualities.

What I learned about leadership after reading Chapter Six is:

_____

_____

_____

_____

_____

STEP TWO

Earn the Leadership badge in this book. Describe for your Girl Scout troop or group or others the action project you completed.

Notes on my action project:

_____

_____

_____

_____

_____

STEP THREE

Earn *one* of the four Junior Girl Scout signs: the Sign of the World (described on page 204), the Sign of the Rainbow, the Sign of the Sun, or the Sign of the Satellite.

To earn the Sign of the _____,

I did these activities:

_____

_____

_____

_____

STEP FOUR

Complete a project that demonstrates your leadership skills. You can choose one of the following or develop your own with your Girl Scout leader's guidance.

1. Do a project that helps others. Investigate the services your community offers and volunteer your time. For example, you could volunteer at a food bank or soup kitchen, build some shelves for a homeless shelter, or repair used toys or make new ones to donate. You could tutor a person in math, reading, or another school subject, or coach a sport you play well.

2. Do a project that helps the environment. Ask your Girl Scout leader for the Contemporary Issues booklet *Earth Matters: A Challenge for Environmental Action* to get ideas for environmental action projects, or check with community groups that are working to protect the environment.

3. Do a project that helps people get along better. Read Chapter Five—Everyone Is Different. Then, plan a community forum to fight prejudice. Contact community groups working in this area and volunteer. Or, participate in a school project on mediation or conflict resolution. Or, see what your neighborhood needs and plan a community project.

4. Do a project that shows girls are great. For example, create a video or other display to foster positive attitudes about girls and women.

INDEX